GOD
IN MY
STORM

GOD
IN MY
STORM

Pamela Williams

CITIOFBOOKS, INC.
3736 Eubank NE Suite A1
Albuquerque, NM 87111-3579
www.citiofbooks.com
Hotline: 1 (877) 389-2759
Fax: 1 (505) 930-7244

Ordering Information:

Quantity sales. Special discounts are available on quantity purchases by corporations, associations, and others. For details, contact the publisher at the address above.

Printed in the United States of America.

ISBN-13:   Paperback   978-1-963209-22-8
              eBook   978-1-963209-24-2
              Hardback   978-1-963209-23-5

Library of Congress Control Number: 2024900279

TABLE OF CONTENTS

DEDICATION

This book exists because of my friendship with Rebekah. She is my God-given sister in Christ. She has been my support, encouragement, teacher, stability, prayer warrior, and closest person to my heart since we were 12 years old. She is my sister in the truest sense of the word.

Everyone should have a Rebekah. She is patient and kind to me at all times. God in His infinite wisdom knew exactly who I was the best person to place squarely in my path to accompany on this most amazing journey. We cannot walk through this life alone which is why God is ever present at our side. When God places an earthly angel to walk with you. It is a blessing to behold.

In my brokenness and sin, I have tried to test and sabotage our friendship. She is aware and pays no attention to my feeble efforts. Those attempts do not even become a topic of discussion. God strategically placed her along with her loving family in my life for a very specific reason. to help me become a better person instead of a chronically bitter one. God, pray and love always win in the end. Never underestimate the power and strength of God and how He cares for us thoughtfully, tirelessly and endlessly.

2 Corinthians 9:15
Thanks be to God for His indescribable gift

Jeremiah 29:11

For I know the plans that I have for you declares the Lord, plans for welfare and not for calamity to give you a future and hope.

Becky and Pam

STORMS

Storms in scripture often represent God's power and amazing presence. When we encounter hardships, difficulties, and personal tragedies in life we respond with similar feelings as God does, such as darkness, lightning, earthquakes, and fire. These are ways God manifests His greatness to us.

Isaiah 25:4
For you have been a stronghold to the poor, a stronghold to the needy in his distress, a shelter from the storm and a shade from the heat; for the breath of the ruthless is like a storm against a wall.

We all experience storms in life. It is in these turbulent times that we wonder and ask, where is God? Why is this happening? Did I do something wrong? Did God make this happen? We actually have the answers in God's Word.

These are some possible reasons:

GOD SEEKS A CONVERSATION WITH US - The Lord speaks gently to our hearts but sometimes He has to increase the volume to be heard. He does this out of love to protect us from our sin.

Romans 15:4
For whatever was written in former days was written for our instruction, that through endurance and through the encouragement of the Scriptures we might have hope.

TO CHANGE OUR DIRECTION - God used a literal storm to get Jonah's attention. We cannot ever avoid God because He is present everywhere.

Jonah 11:2-3
Although the Lord told him to go to Nineveh to "cry against it for their wickedness." Jonah boarded a ship "to flee to Tarshish from the presence of the Lord."

TO ALIGN US CLOSER TO GOD - God is willing to break us in order to glorify Himself to make us more like His Son.

1 Peter 4:13
But rejoice insofar as you share Christ's sufferings, that you may also rejoice and be glad when his glory is revealed.
God who is faithful and just will cause us to seek Him in all storms and when we go astray. He has as many reasons to do so as there are sinners who need His guidance and protection.

Isaiah 54:11
"O afflicted one, storm-tossed and not comforted, behold, I will set your stones in antimony, and lay your foundations with sapphires.

In order to face life's storms we should always remember God's promises to us. Stay in conversation with God and believe in His love for us. Be patient and rely on the faith God has granted each of us.

Philippians 4:19
And my God will supply every need of yours according to his riches in glory in Christ Jesus.

God is with us in every storm. He never abandons us to our sin and wandering. We can be assured by His glorious Words to us.

2 Corinthians 12:9

But he said to me, "My grace is sufficient for you, for my power is made perfect in weakness." Therefore I will boast all the more gladly of my weaknesses, so that the power of Christ may rest upon me.

STRENGTH AND COURAGE
(AUTHOR UNKNOWN)

It takes strength to share a friends pain,
It takes courage to feel your own pain.

It takes strength to hide your own pain,
It takes courage to show it and deal with it.

It takes strength to stand guard,
It takes courage to let your guard down.

It takes strength to conquer,
It takes courage to surrender.

It takes strength to endure abuses,
It takes courage to stop them.

It takes strength to survive,
It takes courage to live.

It takes strength to stand-alone.
It takes courage to lean on a friend.

It takes strength to love,
It takes courage to be loved.

JOB OF LIFE

If you could step into my purple slippers and see how long it's taken me to reconstruct my tiny universe, to include happiness, joy, peace and safety, you would begin to understand how meaningful and protected I now feel. You would also understand why I'm so picky and protective about who I allow into my space at this time. I actively take the time and make the effort to be intentional, thoughtful and respectful towards myself.

It has taken the majority of my life to let myself experience this comfort and safety that never was mine in the beginning. Creatively it is to my liking and style. In my living space, every inch feels like me. I've never experienced something completely mine, designed by me, where I feel safe and comfortable.

I've become conceited by the world's definition but really, I'm celebrating myself by caring for my emotional needs in an effort to be present in my "Living Hope" ministry and for others who may have an emotional need. I'm driven to help people begin to break away from all the things that are keeping them stuck.

I am speaking my truth with some fear and trepidation, but my goal is for others to see themselves and perhaps know someone close to them with similar complexities acquired as a result of abuse and trauma.

In speaking my truth in such a vulnerable and personal way, there may be people described in unflattering ways on these pages. I know longer protect abusers of any kind. In fact, if you read about yourself in an unflattering way on these pages and do not find yourself warmly remembered, that is not my fault. I can't change the facts. Those people should have behaved better.

Accordingly, I'm working hard at setting boundaries in my relationships. I'm also not sustaining and keeping one sided relationship on life support any longer. I'm seeking reciprocal friendships. There have been so many of my friendships that are one sided that I've always made myself available for, that I have felt disingenuous in those relationships. I never say no. I make all the phone calls and arrange to do things. I carry the friendships; I do heavy lifting. Not anymore though. I'm practicing peace.

I've actually made a bold decision to end all one-sided relationships. Also, to eliminate all toxic relationships that are held together by my efforts alone. God has been allowing for new friendships in my space.

Newly armed with what is best and emotionally safe for me has equipped me with a significant understanding of just who I should let into my universe. God has provided a much-needed healing gift where boundaries come more naturally and with more clarity.

Proverbs 20:24
A person's steps are directed by the Lord. How can anyone understand they're own way?

THANKS AND GRATITUDE

I'd like to thank all of God's special angels, who He personally has enlisted to accompany me on my life's journey and teach me what love is and isn't about. What new genuine happiness feels like. How to understand my emotions and keep them in check and most importantly, how to navigate the healing path I've been on.

It's been a harrowing journey with much mental illness on board and deep sorrow about my condition in this world. Understanding my inability to see around corners or my hyper vigilance about all the wrong things. Missteps, mistakes and mishaps.

Throughout my life I've been desperately seeking love and understanding along with a sense of well-being and satisfaction with who I am. That eluded me for 67 years. I repeatedly pursued people who I was never going to be good enough for. Simply because they were the wrong person. We will not be valued and loved by the wrong person. God is always the right person.

I'd also like to thank my abusers. Their impact on my life has been learning to embrace perseverance, determination and a quest for mental wellness and stability. I did not intend for my abusers and tormentors to have a lifelong negative impact on me. I wanted more from my life. I wanted contentment and peace. I needed God's healing hand for that.

I wasted and lost many years, regretting my past and wishing against hope for it to never happen. Trying to make sense out of the insanity and vilifying all the players who negatively impacted my world including myself. I was pursuing the wrong thing. Simply placing blame where it belonged and having the strength to confront my tormentors was not an answer. That is looking outward instead of inward to my heart for relief. It is also leaving God out of the picture.

Now I embrace the past I previously swore to hate. I've learned lessons in life no one could ever teach me due to those invaluable experiences. It created a person I could never imagine into existence. I've become a brave, strong and more resilient person who is deeply in love with God. God was always by my side, though at the time I didn't notice Him and His handy work in my life. I often wondered where He was.

God, who is all powerful and the creator of all things, is also the re-creator. The God who can clean up our mess, neatly fold down the corners, press the seams and MAKE YOU NEW IN CHRIST, is always present. That is a miraculous thing. Instead of hiding, pointing fingers and trying to heal myself, I could let God go to work without constantly holding Him on the side for rainy days and emergencies only.

My favorite word is crap. I use it again and again and overuse it regularly. To those who love me and put up with endless amounts of CRAP from me, you are loved more than you know. You stayed the course. You didn't fall for all the attempts I made to sabotage our relationship and/ or friendship. You didn't judge my survival and trauma behaviors as personal attacks on you but as an ongoing poverty of my soul. You prayed faithfully for me on the difficult and miraculous journey through my life and it's not over yet!

Carl, Marjorie, William and Rebekah, Dave and Mary, and Chris my PT extraordinaire. These were my heavy hitters. In for the long haul. Open to God's call, they faithfully prayed and showed up. A difficult gift to simply be there. It's generous and unselfish to give your time and listening skills along with empathy to others. These angels have been there for me over a span of 17 to 58 years. They never once abandoned me or injured my heart in any way. I never felt a moment of insecurity with them. They just loved me with a supernatural love that only God could sustain.

It is said that in life, we pick our own therapists. Not the ones with degrees but the ones we meet and trust along the way. Each of these people has played an important role for me. Each met a need. Each answered a call. Each has taught me lessons and has shown me kindness, patience and love. I have loved them in return.

If you have as many as seven dedicated and loving friends willing to show up and be there for you, God is blessing your life and heart enormously. Praise and thank Him in a kneeling position!

Second string, but equally as important are Elizabeth, Tina, Debra, Pamela, Pastor Todd (who when I sought his counsel on feeling like I should leave my church because of conflicts said, without skipping a beat, "I'll miss you") I genuinely miss his boldness and sarcasm.

Jan, Gloria, Ed, Robert and James. This group dared to befriend me and in doing so taught me stability. James gave me a run for my money, expected me to work hard and gave me homework. He was in my life a few short months but worked my behind off. I had to admit I'd finally encountered someone who was smarter than me.

His assignments for me were writing to explore or explain something in therapy. When I showed up my pages were printed out. He then asked if he could share them with other clients. One good important thing about Robert and James who were my therapy team and never placated me, glossed over things, let me get away with nonsense and saw something more in me than I could imagine on my own. They knew I was hungry for change and willing to listen and do the necessary work required.

The only relative I have an ongoing relationship with is my aunt Sharron. We love each other deeply and argue frequently. She's the baby in her family. We're eight years apart in age. I jokingly tell people I raised her. People erroneously believe me.

I tell her almost everything and she keeps a lot from me. We're damaged. She came from the same destructive dysfunctional family I did. We are all we have left of people in our family we feel free to be vulnerable and open with. It's risky for sure. Trust doesn't come easily when you don't know who you can trust. I abhor lying. She lies a lot. Sometimes I let it hurt because it does. Other times I let it pass because I know her lies are also her truth. Separating it out is like an amputation.

All these individuals were and have been a stabilizing force who heard me and didn't run away. All my well-played sabotage techniques were ignored. Their love and prayers kept me rising on eagles' wings and still do.

There are so many more dear friends that it would take a lifetime to mention. You came in and out of my life, did a little or accomplished much. You may have loved, hated, abused, antagonized, or even tortured me. But you were each a catalyst that played a huge part in my walk. I wanted to be more than just another misfit raised by vermin.

I'm now stronger, smarter and more willing to deal with cleaning out the cobwebs and demons that weigh me down. Everyone I've encountered in life was a lesson to be learned. Each individual inspired me in a very specific way to stand tall. God is with each of you always.

A monster wasn't created from the ashes of my life. Instead, a clever genius emerged. Too smart for the enemy who tried to dominate my world with pain and failures, too many to mention.

Friends, even wolves in sheep's clothing, have lessons to teach us along the way. No experience is pointless or useless. God works everything for our good.

God is our FATHER. He is raising us as His own. That entails love and discipline. We are after all saints and sinners. As God's children, we require guidance and a firm but patient hand. God is perfect in that capacity because everything He does is perfect.

Do not ever stay stuck in your past. Yes, it becomes part of your DNA. It lives in your bones and has your brain wired on auto pilot responses. Instead, make a choice to heal. There is no specific timetable for healing. Our wounds are not the same. It's not a competition and our paths are uniquely our own. Seek the Father in everything. He will never disappoint you. He chose you before you were ever conceived. Choose God and choose to be a clever genius.

CLEVER-quick to understand, learn and devise or apply ideas. Intelligent. Skilled at doing or achieving something talented.

GENIUS-exceptional intellectual or creative power or other natural ability. Natural creativity in general or some specific event.

Marjorie and Carl Moline. Loved and prayed for me since I was twelve.

CRAP HAPPENS

That's my favorite word again. "Crap..." Maybe if we listen carefully, we can hear crap happening. Because crap happens again and again. Can we ever escape crap? Why does crap always happen to me?

There is a rampant and unfortunate fallacy in many religions that believe "Christians should not have any problems." I've been told by well-meaning sisters in Christ, that my illnesses are a result of my "lack of faith.". I've also been told that "bad" things happen in my world because I'm not in the Word enough. I could easily deny their accusations and prove the amount of time spent on God's Word. I write daily devotionals. My process for that is to utilize the 29 different Bibles I have along with my reference books and substantial monitors and observers of faith. As I'm made to be dismissed. We must be very careful blaming victims for their circumstances.

Others condemn people with difficulties for not having enough prayer time. It is reported that people with "crap" taking place are being punished by God who is withholding His blessings to teach a lesson. This is meant to be encouragement for good Christians and an incentive to pray for Devine deliverance from these demonic assaults. Others simply believe and confess that God is doing this to them or has allowed this to happen to them. The exact source and cause for such trials in life has long been argued and there are numerous positions taken on this topic depending on your religious theology. Some refer to it as just "bad luck," or an illusion to be disregarded. It's just Murphy's law, bad karma, or my favorite "the fickle finger of fate." We are in the world but not of the world. It is quite natural to expect that "crap" is going to happen to us in our lifetime.

John 12:31
Now is the time for judgment on this world; now the prince of this world will be driven out.

There is a unique and efficient system put in place by the ruler of this world. God's system prevails among all mankind as God has orchestrated it. We were not promised perfection in paradise. To be exact, what we have been assured are trials and tribulations. It is expected that we will be rejected by selfish, broken people. Our exact promise is that you will not be tested beyond what you are able. Do not let well-meaning, often spiritually confused fellow sinners interpret your predicaments and pronounce the calamities you're experiencing all your fault.

Do not misunderstand God's Word. We will most assuredly reap what we sow as consequences of sin. However, we must be an encouragement to one another, not their accusers, when hardships occur. It is not our place to ask them to repent of whatever crime they committed that brought them hardship. Sin brings with it natural consequences. God's forgiveness, unbinds and frees us to move ahead with repentant hearts to serve and love one another.

1 Corinthians 10:13
There hath no temptation taken you, but such as is common to man: but God is faithful, who will not suffer you to be tempted above that you are able; but will with temptation also make way a way to escape, that you may be able to bear it.

Have confidence in God's promises and do not fall prey to the notion that as believers we should not be experiencing tragedies, aggravations, inconveniences, and crises in a fallen world. We are all sinners! We will be victims of sin for certain. There is no escape because we call ourselves Christians. As Christians, our trials illustrate our inability and insufficiency to save ourselves and the need for our Savior. This is no different for non-Christians. Christians on the other hand have the security of the One who has come to give us eternal life.

We must also resist attributing sinful actions to God Himself. Although God is the Creator and sustainer and deliberate cause of all things in creation, He is not to be blamed as the cause of evil. Evil is contrary to God's character.

1 Peter 4:12
friends, do not be surprised at the fiery ordeal that has come on you to test you, as though something strange.

Crap Happens

CARE INSTRUCTIONS

I like to write about things that come up in conversation that I can learn more about through the written word. I will also write about myself and how I like to be treated. This seemed like an important endeavor during the writing process but afterward, when I read it over, it seemed like I was putting a lot of responsibility on people around me regarding my behavior instead of taking responsibility for myself. While letting people know how you wish to be treated and setting boundaries are important to establish, expecting others to put up with your dysfunctional behaviors is asking too much.

The following explanations and antidotes seem informed and logical, however, it's not other people's job to be mindful of my needs. It's squarely my responsibility.

I'm pretty specific about how I wish to be treated by others. I know myself well. I may not tell you how to treat me, but you'll eventually discover there's a problem when I'm no longer there. I will most likely avoid you or delete you altogether.

As a victim of every form of abuse, I can't stand being judged. Most people don't like it, but that's an angry pain that shreds my heart. No one has walked in my shoes. There is no way to impart enough information to anyone that would satisfy any understanding of what took place.

The pain I've lugged around through life has been emotionally and physically intense and exhausting. My body is very sick from abuse. It has taken the brunt of my trauma.

I need people surrounding me who are flexible and understanding. I don't respond well or tolerate passive- aggressive behavior. I'll eventually resent you and dislike you. That opinion is not likely to ever change. My memory is long and detailed. It's not a punishment towards you, it's a survival skill for me.

I need people who are capable of being honest in a loving way. Honesty is highly prized. I require it in all my relationships. If I find out you've lied to me, I will not be in your life. There is only one person who lies to me that I stay in a relationship. I put up with her purely out of love and sorrow.

I tolerate her dishonesty because we are cut from the same cloth. She does not work on her stuff but avoids, stuff, hides, and is not honest. This is how she survives her trauma. I cope with her issues and refuse to be her babysitter. That's how we survive with each other.

I can be impulsive and even inattentive. It's easy for me to hurt people's feelings and I need to be reeled back in on those occasions.

I work hard at self-awareness but sometimes I'm clueless. My behavior does not always match my intentions because of difficulty with interpersonal skills.

I talk a lot and it's good to know when I'm monopolizing a conversation or interrupting too much. This behavior is primarily anxiety-driven. Let me know when this is happening without sarcasm.

Everyone wants to be liked, including me. I place importance on friends who find out my strengths and values instead of focusing on my weaknesses.

Unsolicited advice is unwanted and ignored. When sharing or venting, I want someone to "listen" only. A generous gift that is often a challenge for the giver. We are prone to fix and rescue. This behavior has nothing to do with helping someone. It's really an attempt to rescue ourselves from our discomfort with your problems.

I fear conflict, rejection, and aggression. I'm a Fawn. I work hard to smooth things out. I can easily disassociate and/or become catatonic around rage or violence. I'm often hopelessly overwhelmed in many complicated situations.

Maintaining friendships and jobs is an admitted struggle. I was raised by wolves. I'm bad at interacting. I read social cues well but sometimes ignore them and regret it later. Different processes that move me forward. More so than average people who weren't raised by wolves.

I have much to contribute, enthusiasm, creativity, energy, humor, intuition, sensitivity, empathy, and more. I have intense anxiety and am never certain of anything. Buying expensive items causes me physical illness.

I often need help with decision-making and money management. I struggle in social situations and am an introvert. I can have emotional outbursts when I'm feeling overwhelmed and in the face of rage or intense conflict, I simply shut down.

My brain works differently due to trauma and abuse. I can obsessively ruminate about anything. I come with lots of guilt and shame that amplifies when I'm feeling insecure. I apologize a lot, even without reason. I always feel like a bother and/or burden to others, so I resist asking for help. I blame myself when things go wrong even if it doesn't involve me. Sometimes life feels impossible for me.

I'm as passionate as I am flighty. I crave stability and change (I have to rearrange a lot). I must be heard. I seek out validation but can accept when I'm wrong. I write it ALL down (in journals, emails, and texts) then regret when I hit send or allow others access to things too personal to share.

I love easily and passionately but can be emotionally disconnected at times. I distrust or trust too easily. I frequently complain and sound negative but that doesn't mean I am. There is nothing wrong with being negative. Chronic negativity is a different issue. Positive people often exhaust me. I have difficulty picking safe people in my life as friends and confidants. I can easily overshare, and this often leaves me emotionally exposed. Boundaries can often be a blur.

I'm slow to recognize abuse before I can escape or stop it. I'm prone to obsessing but can sometimes reign it in with self- awareness. I'm a loyal and loving friend for life when loved in return.

I am not just the total of my illnesses, physical or psychological. I exist apart from them and am worthy of love.

These issues have plagued me forever. I'm adept at integrating them with the proper trauma responses. It has taken 68 years of hard work to retrain my brain to react differently. I'm still practicing and am always eager for new challenges.

Victims instinctively do what is necessary to survive their abuse. We learn so well that the behavior (trauma responses) becomes indistinguishable as dysfunctional and becomes our normal.

I spent years trying to make people realize the extent of my abuse and pain. I hoped that the reasons behind the behavior would cause others to be empathetic and kind to me. That rarely happened. I have no such expectations any longer.

Looking back, I now realize I was expecting a pass on bad behavior. I used my trauma as the reason I had so many relationship difficulties and expected to be loved unconditionally by everyone. That thinking didn't require me to change myself, but I expected to change others in the way they viewed and treated me.

Now I take responsibility for myself and work hard to heal instead of retelling the story over and over. That pattern only served to reinforce my resolve to stay mentally unhealthy and garner sympathy. It's easy and comfortable to remain a victim. No one can blame you. There is another way to learn important changes in your life that can bring hope and joy into your world. There is nothing written that state's victims must stay that way forever. You can never forget your past, but you can learn new coping strategies that are healthier than trauma responses.

If you see yourself in these words, you are not alone. This describes each of us from time to time. We're all prone to the realities, difficulties, and complexities of navigating life.

Our difficult experiences can either dominate, run, and/or ruin our lives. Another scenario is to surrender to God, confess our need for Him, and take responsibility to work at wellness along with becoming obedient to His will.

God is ever-present and lovingly nudging us into more confident growth. He's not above having us repeat as many times as needed the important lessons we face.

If you find yourself in a difficult spot emotionally and you tend to run, chances are you are right where God can help you work through the problem. If you choose to avoid the issue, I have no doubt you will have other opportunities to visit it again.

He wants to ease our pain and suffering. Without letting go of our defensive attitudes and behaviors and being real about these actions derailing our lives instead of happily advancing us, we cannot grow. We will stay root bound and miserably uncomfortable.

All of that dysfunction creates further insecurity, depression and anxiety. We will have difficulty in our love relationship with God too. Lack of trust, second guessing God and avoiding His truth will ensue. It will be difficult to have any kind of relationship with Him that is much different from our relationship to the world. We are always safe in His capable hands.

With recognition comes responsibility. The truth can be an uncomfortable and challenging blessing but may not feel like it at the time. God does not supply the truth and then abandons us on our own. He is lifting us up and holding us tightly, guiding us into His light.

FILTERED BEAUTY

Recently, I've been experimenting with photo filter apps on my phone. Ones that change your age from older to younger or the reverse. You can even make yourself a cartoon character.

I was amazed and stunned into silence by the results. I found myself staring at a beautiful woman. I began obsessively using the filter on all my pictures. It was me I saw as stunning.

In my mind, I had always been ugly, made fun of, and bullied because I was so unattractive. I had a wandering left eye, and yellow teeth from medication my mother took while pregnant with me. I also had an extra canine tooth which caused crowding and left one tooth behind another creating a traffic jam in my mouth. This caused me much embarrassment and I refused to smile when I remembered my self-consciousness about it.

I was ugly, there was no doubt. I was also a trauma victim. The person I saw in the mirror was not recognizable to me. I often looked through and past my image as if I were invisible. The same way I felt in life.

My brain translated my image or God-given beauty into someone I could no longer stand to see. My reflection was a blob of indescribable nothing. I could however still feel and experience the pain of my existence in my innermost being. That deep emotional pain played heavily into the distorted view I had of my image.

With all the trauma I've experienced in life, my self-esteem didn't stand a chance along with the physical flaws and helplessness about who I thought I was. I honestly did not know who I was and it was difficult to find answers in my emotionally dishonest and void family.

Victims have their internal filter by which they view themselves. It is one of misperception, distortion, and lies. Victims generally see themselves as damaged, ugly, unlovable, unwanted, dumb, helpless, hated, unworthy, and ultimately lost.

It's hard to see your beauty when broken, hurt, and numb. God is seeking that brokenness and longs to restore our beauty, bring us rest, heal our souls and in the process, rediscover and reclaim His lost sheep.

We were created by Him from love, to be loved and to love in return. Allow God to uncover, unburden, and return you to the beauty he began in you, seen through His eyes.

God our creator longs to change our countenance along with providing peace and joy to our souls. He wants you to see yourself through His filter, not through yours or the world's. Let Him.

God has lovingly guided me into His waiting arms. He is good and faithful to relentlessly pursue what He loves most. Us. To be created and sought after by perfection Himself is daunting to victims. We've lost our ability to trust which no longer has any value. God has the perfect filter with which to gaze upon His creation. We are created in His image. Looking into the eyes of another, we are getting glimpses of Christ. That is nothing less than beautiful.

Filtered Beauty   Unfiltered

WHEN FEAR IS YOUR NORMAL

Imagine never feeling safe. Never sure of anything or anyone. What if you never had a space that was yours, except for cement floors and walls? Not yours either but the closest you ever came to having your own space. The cold unfinished basement in our dismal home was my room. By choice.

Our basement was a self-imposed exile and oasis. It was how I escaped the chaos, scary unpredictable minutia, and rampant evil of my everyday existence. I preferred the empty uninviting space with no heat or air conditioning over the hell that existed above my head.

It's difficult never even having your own "personal space". That all-important space that extends between 1 1/2 ft. and 4 ft. from your body. Your entitled space, your safety net, and reasonable boundary. Any "space" I could garner was well coveted and well-earned.

Think about how you'd feel being forced to greet and hug your sex abuser as a child because he was married to your mom's favorite aunt. These were the relatives they fawned over. Additionally, I had to hug all adult relatives and family friends, never knowing if they were abusers or not. Wondering if they're sizing me up and/or grooming me for later.

What if those hugs always felt like you were being "violated?" If that forced physical contact with others frightened, you to your core and left you wanting to flee or get a bath. A bath that washed away all the dirtiness and nastiness of unwanted human contact. That made you sick to your stomach and anxiety ridden. Forcing children to give hugs and kisses to adults is a violation of them and a practice that needs to end.

It didn't take much to make me feel dirty. Being desired and sought after like a box of chocolate candy pretty much did the job for me. Feeling dirty came naturally alongside the ongoing belief that I was bad. That doesn't require much examination. A child connects the dots to all that surrounds them. It's all about them. I was used and abused. Stripped of my innocence and dignity against my will. Of course, that had to mean I was bad. Why else would all this sordid drama be taking over my life? The trauma and abuse distorted my inner moral compass and understanding of right and wrong. These issues were overlapping. Being bad had to be the explanation.

When you are young, you don't understand why bad things happen or how things can hurt so badly. You just think it must be you. That there is something fundamentally wrong with you. You don't have a way to gauge the big picture. Your awareness doesn't include the fact that your parents might not have any idea what they're doing. That quite possibly they were getting everything wrong, and you deserved better. That their childhood damage was now becoming their childhood damage and misery.

Fear and distrust occupied my mind and subconscious thoughts regularly. I was always second-guessing myself and everyone around me. Sounds chaotic? I couldn't rely on my good judgment as I had none. I was always trying to gauge my danger level. I lived life with the notion I was never safe. Simply because I never was. I was easy prey. I didn't protest, cry or scream. I kept quiet and protected my abusers.

The fear and distrust I felt had left me sitting alone at home much of the time as a child. I missed many special holiday occasions and parties.

I'd been lied to so many times about where we were going, that I simply stopped going anywhere.

If I was being forced to go somewhere, I had a strategy to avoid that too. Always being told to stay clean before leaving for an event, I headed for the nearest dirt pile and or mud I could find. There I intentionally applied dirt to my clothes. It worked more often than not but also came with a spanking.

I was tricked into going places many times over. The cycle of abuse pushed past my boundaries so frequently that I no longer wished to be involved in anything, or go anywhere. I'd rather sit home by myself than be caught in a trap. Predictably, I became trapped like a rat in my self-created bubble. While earnestly trying to not be trapped by others, I locked myself away, becoming more and more reclusive and inward.

This delicate dance started at age three. I'm now sixty-eight and still unraveling my dangerous past. Still two-stepping through life, but now as a smarter well-seasoned pro.

I lost many years, regretting the past, wishing against hope it had never happened. Trying to make sense out of insanity and vilifying everyone including myself.

Now I accept my past. I learned lessons in my life that could not have been learned any other way. No one could teach that harsh reality, it had to be lived.

That life created a person I could never imagine into existence. A strong, independent woman who faces adversity and problems head-on. A lifelong learner who has a large appetite for God's Word. I've stopped longing for a past I never had and started embracing the one I do.

God, who is all-powerful and creator of all things, is also the re- creator. The God who can clean up your mess, neatly wash out your sin, fold down the corners, and press the seams can also "MAKE YOU NEW IN CHRIST."

My favorite word is crap. I use it and overuse it regularly. CRAP happens. Residual CRAP is the byproduct of CRAP. I even keep track of CRAP on lists of CRAP. Your CRAP doesn't have to always stink up the place. Clean up your CRAP!

It's been an interesting journey, full of twists, turns, avoidance, and all manners of pain and psychological games. There was always humor too. Humor is what kept me coherent and upright for the most part. I welcome people to my party. I have amazing, unbelievable stories to tell. All for God's glory.

A monster wasn't created from all the emotional and physical destruction in my life, a clever genius emerged. Too smart for the enemy who tried to dominate my world with pain and sorrow. Satan whispered in my ear over and endlessly, that God did not love me. Satan can't wait to work his lies into our hearts and tear our eyes and focus away from God. He picks at our wounds till they fester with infection.

Never forget that in our Baptism, we are marked by the sign of the cross and we are God's. Satan would have us forget who we are and to whom we belong and question God's love and support in our trials and suffering.

Our suffering is not a result of God not doing His job as a father to protect us. Our suffering is a result of sin. Mine, yours, and collectively the worlds. It's important to understand this distinction. There is a choice to be made here. The choice to believe, trust, and cling to God's Word or the decision to believe the lies and betrayals of Satan.

Choose to be a clever genius. Change course. God is with you and wants your head well. He's in the healing business. His hospital is huge.

My story is real, miraculous, sad, and joyous. You may find yourself in it, as we are all victims of that ever-present nagging human condition, SIN! Our way through sin and life, and salvation from it, is God and God alone.

This truly is a story about my life but I'm not the story. God is. He is the author of life. He is always in control. His love saves us all. Apart from Him, we are nothing.

Heneverletsusgo!

STRUGGLING AGAINST BEING BAD

I am often aware that I'm behaving badly or in a maladaptive way. I don't like that I do this but still, it occurs. I never feel good about it and sometimes apologize when it's blatantly unacceptable behavior. Other times I feel very bad about myself and the more I stew in it the worse I feel. This starts a vicious cycle of spiraling down into what I call "the darkness." I go there quite easily. Sometimes it takes days, weeks, months, or years to get there. Some days I'm only seconds from that cold, desolate place where I feel like a hostage.

I struggle terribly with the feeling that I'm basically BAD. I won't just take responsibility for what I do wrong, but I'll take responsibility for the wrongs that were done to me by others. I take on responsibility for the bad behavior of others and try to smooth everything over to keep the peace.

I hate conflict and meanness. I work hard to remedy it, even if you're the source of the problem. I'm embarrassed by the bad behavior of others and sarcastically excuse this behavior with humor. There are no winners with this deplorable conduct and I become the enabler when I don't take a stand against it.

I hate these scenarios yet am like a moth to a flame. This is familiar territory for me. I understand my role and I'm good at it. I'm a Fawn. I straighten out the mess, dry everyone's tears, and am the calm and comedy relief in the storm. I clean up the scene of the crime but more importantly, keep the instigator out of serious trouble. Then show up again for rinse and repeat.

This always makes me feel bad. It's much like riding shotgun in the robber's get away car. I'm going to go to jail if we're caught even if I didn't know a robbery was taking place. Hanging around with robbers is not a good deal for me. In doing so repeatedly, I'm reinforcing the idea of how bad I am. Bad people hang with other bad people.

I even punish myself for being bad. I have several methods I use regularly. I overeat, overspend, and make poor choices. These behaviors only temporarily numb my feelings of being bad. Then I'm left to deal with the consequences of my punishment strategy.

I've been traveling down this rabbit hole in earnest since 1/10/19. The day I worked very hard to die. I'm generally punishing myself by being self-destructive and self-sabotaging. This keeps the internal argument going about how bad I am. A vicious cycle of badness.

My only escape from this cycle of conviction is pushing it all out of my mind. I stop staring at it because staring at it hurts and I feel like I have to have a reasonable solution to fix it of which I have none.

I respond to my behavior and feelings with hatred, deep sorrow, intense fear, a sense of loss and abandonment along with the need to run away and hide from the world. It is difficult to live with all that negativity in your head. This is also how I envision others view me too.

I justify and convince myself I'm unlovable and too BAD to be in a relationship with anyone. These feelings continue to intensify until I simply can't take the horrible pressure of how bad I am.

I am easily driven by my badness to try and be EXTRA good. I never want to offend someone or disappoint anyone to counteract my badness.

I can live with the fact I can't please everyone and not everyone likes me to the point of distraction. I internalize the prospect of not being perfect with the fact that I'm bad. I'm bad because I'm damaged. I live with lots of fear of being found out and exposed for being bad. What will I do when I'm caught??

It's so frustrating because I really work hard at improving myself along with my self-esteem and yet still fall into a shameful heap of feeling BAD.

As a trauma victim who also has symptoms of anger, unresponsiveness, depression, anxiety, and emotional outbursts. It's not helpful to feel these things as they too condemn me as being BAD.

Another way I reinforce this is to make a statement and add a tagline about how stupid I am to it. It's a bad habit my aunt pointed out to me. I'm using my stepfather's words on myself now that he's dead. I wasn't even consciously aware of doing it.

I'm a quagmire of feelings. I easily assume other people's unhappiness, conflict, and disappointment. I don't have enough negativity, so I'll take on yours too. These "add-ons" really serve the purpose of keeping me trapped in my BADNESS also.

I live in constant conflict, trying to be who I am, have my desires, and meet everyone else's expectations of me. That conflict keeps me feeling bad too. I have lots of behaviors, thoughts, and reactions that keep the dysfunction functioning well. I'm the saboteur queen. Even if someone is mad at me or disappointed, I'll assume it's all because I'm a bad person. I work hard at fixing broken things. I need to let go of trying to fix things I didn't break. Situations are broken, people are broken, I see brokenness everywhere but it's not my job.to mend brokenness. That job is squarely on God.

I never attribute a problem to someone else or take ownership of another mess I didn't create. That job belongs on God's capable shoulders too.

I also feel bad when good things happen to me. I cautiously anticipate it soon going bad because I'm a bad person. Nothing good is ever going to last.

I can't begin to describe the destruction this thought process has on me. I am never safe in my skin. It's like being a fugitive on the run. Sooner or later, I'll get caught, tried, and hung for being very BAD. Can one move and grow beyond the bonds of BADNESS? Is God big enough for that job?

Maladaptive behavior does not allow me to see a clear path to my future desires. This affects many areas of my life including relationships, work, education, and self-esteem. My most used maladaptive behavior is avoidance. I use that most when looking at my behavior. I do this to lessen the fall into the darkness. When in the darkness, nothing in my world is any longer predictable. I just hung on for the ride. Bad things are about to begin when the darkness descends.

This is so frightening to me I just work hard to not go there. I fear I will self-destruct if I do. That is more pain than already exists for me consciously. It becomes too much to bear at times. Death is preferable.

Surely God has a plan for me in this area too. As I write about these difficulties in my life, these words I write begin to paint a clearer picture of the problem and I desperately seek solutions for my problematic existence.

I have never truly been myself around others as I don't have a clear picture of who I am. As a result, I have never seen evidence that any part of who I am is lovable and worthy. That is a difficult place to be stuck in. The only hope of unraveling the massive ball of barbed wire is Christ.

I'm trusting in Faith, Hope, and God's Love.

MORE BAD

It's difficult to stop the rush of feelings I have connected to being bad. So, I decided not to stop them and let them float to the surface.

Much of the trauma I experienced and the ways I was tortured are unimaginable and I cannot speak of them. It physically hurts me to relive them in my mind. The guilt I feel for being a victim is overwhelming.

I had to be BAD or these events would never have occurred. As a teenager and young adult, I engaged in risky behaviors, and that caused a lot of traumas for me because of the dangerous situations I put myself in.

When horrible things ensued, I blamed myself for being in a position to allow terrible things to take place. I never placed the blame on the perpetrators.

I went along with everything. I was usually drunk or high and was not resistant to much of what was done to me. Many times, I was unconscious.

Sometimes I protested but that always resulted in things escalating to get me to comply. The torture increased over time. When you are being tortured, it's the most degrading and humiliating experience to go through. There is a helplessness that takes over. I tried and tried to understand why and how I got into these situations and always arrived at the same conclusion. Just me being treated badly because I'm bad.

I couldn't fight back. I did not have that in me. I truly was convinced things could only get worse if I were to fight back. Death was a constant concern for me.

I ALWAYS took the blame onto myself for whatever crime was perpetrated against me. It never occurred to me to report and prosecute those who harmed me. This is how and why I try to avoid getting stuck in BAD. It's very painful. It makes me want to get in my car and simply disappear.

The thoughts are still so vivid and real, live exposed in my mind. I cannot stop the thought that I should not be alive. I don't deserve to be here.

Bad people must die or be in jail forever. They must not be allowed to inflict their badness on anyone.

Bad people destroy others. They ruin children for life. They are dangerous to everyone. They are a blight on humanity. They're evil and thoughtless. They're hostile and insulting. They deeply wound and exploit the innocent. They hate.

It begins to occur to me that I'm describing my stepfather along with myself to a much lesser degree. Was I created by George? Molded by his hatred and sickness into a person with his characteristics? That would be the ultimate insult. To be his victim and become a perpetrator born out of his sickness and hatred for me.

I believe in my mind's eye; I am like him. I have to fight hard against the part of me that came to resemble him. I frequently think to myself that I do not deserve to live or interact with others. My pain and shame are too big to handle. It is taking my life from me. It has always been doing that. One painful breath at a time my life leaves me.

This is a can of worms I don't like to open. These feelings don't need the light of day upon them. Any good I ever accomplished could not erase or hide the BAD that has ensued.

What has been done to me has the biggest hold on me. I can never escape the cruelty, torture, humiliation, and degradation done to me. It's as if "I" did not matter or count for anything.

I was as meaningless and useless as roadkill. I have been treated as such and tortured, beaten, and left to die. I've been left to die many times. It makes no sense that I'm still living.

I desperately try to put a meaningful life together for myself as I mature but my past has a stranglehold on me. Escape seems impossible but I have determination and a goal of peace.

I don't believe that there is a solution for being BAD or that anything could work against it. That is why I have no desire to look at my badness. Not because I choose not to, it just seems an impossible and hopeless cause. It hurts too much.

With God, our sins are forgiven. We are not required to forgive ourselves. God supplies all the forgiveness that we need at all times.

We can move beyond the negativity in our lives. We don't have to understand it, stuff it, or justify it. We simply have to hand it to God.

Matthew 6:14-15
For if you forgive others for their transgressions, your heavenly Father will also forgive you. But if you do not forgive men, then your heavenly Father will not forgive your transgressions.

THE BIG DEAL ABOUT BEING SMART

I'm incredibly smart (clever genius) and do not take criticism well. That does not mean I can't admit when I'm wrong, it simply means if I'm criticized, it might be kinder to just shoot me dead. A monumental pain wrapped in self-defeat eats at the very core of my being, under the weight of criticism. That very criticism, large or small, is all the evidence required to condemn my existence. Criticism isn't about getting something wrong; it speaks to my incompetence, foolishness, and lack of self-worth.

It hurts because I've generally explored everything thoroughly that comes out of my mouth. I do so not to be wrong. I'm not prone to speaking about or giving my opinion on information that I've not thoroughly researched. I never want to look stupid. I work hard as a lifelong student, to be well-rehearsed and knowledgeable on important topics.

It's not that there is something wrong with being wrong, it's that in my brain the only noise I hear when I'm being criticized, is run, hide, and isolate. Out of that comes self-loathing and condemnation. I punish myself for being dumb.

Growing up, I was criticized for just about everything. I was told I was an elephant. In actuality, I was the skinniest kid in the house and on our block. My poetry was criticized along with my drawings. I sought acceptance mostly from my evil stepfather. He was never going to praise me for anything and yet I consistently sought his approval.

One of my worst triggers is looking stupid. I was made to feel stupid growing up but in actuality, I'm the smartest in my family. I secretly believed I was all alone. My mother used to tell me repeatedly to stop thinking so much, as I was always curiously questioning my world.

To prove that I was smart, I purchased I.Q. tests that all of us siblings took together. It was a rare occasion that we were congregated in one spot at the same time. I scored the highest on the test. I wasn't just a clever genius; I truly am a genius.

Armed with proof of my intelligence has not made me feel more secure. I still live with the feelings of stupidity and my aunt frequently describes me as the smartest dumb person she knows. Yes, that is abusive, especially in light of my insecurity about that topic. No compliment can ever be given without a dig or criticism attached to it in my family. No one escapes the family's backhanded way compliments are given.

I realize no one in my family will ever admit that I know anything or have any special knowledge of something. It goes against their narrative. They would have to change and that, my friends, is a dirty word in our family. Truthfully, I believe I'm scared of my family. I'm cut from the same cloth but not at all the same patterns. I'm open to change and self-evaluation. I want my life to be different and God-centered. I actively work on my problems. This does not make me perfect or better than others, it makes me different.

I'm struggling to let go of their emotional hold on me. That includes their approval and validation.

When my mother died, I was with her. Her firstborn was the only child to be with her. When I realized she had taken her last breath and was no longer among the living, I crawled into her bed and lay across her chest sobbing uncontrollably.

This went on for three long hours. During this time, I received phone calls from each of my children and my ex-husband pleading with me to get off grandma. The sorrow and pain I felt was an accumulation of 65 years of pain, longing and loss.

The tears I shed did not have anything to do with the death of my mother. They had everything to do with the death of my hope. My mother's death finalized any hope I had that she would ever apologize to me or thank me for all I'd done for her or lastly that she would ever say the words to me "I love you."

She was gone. Most likely she never would have done any of those things for me anyway, but now that she was dead, I had to let go of my fantasy and accept it would never be a possibility.

My mother true to form, had the last laugh too. She left what little money she had to my drunk fowl-mouthed sister, who had laid eyes on my mother exactly once in the previous twenty years. It was not important to me to be left with any money. However, the significance of who she left it to be a definite kick in my rear. It was designed to be an insult to me, which showed her lack of respect or appreciation for me.

What she was saying to me was that she had genuine disappointment in me, as I'd become less agreeable to her manipulations, less accepting of her lies, and not as easy to control through blatant shame tactics. I was getting well, and that scared her and made her feel insecure and unsettled.

In that, I can be seen as threatening to my entire family. It used to hurt me deeply that I was not respected for being who I am. Now I don't care so much. I stopped beating my head against the proverbial brick wall, in favor of choosing to love and accepting myself as I am. I don't need validation from my dysfunctional family to be well. Deciding to cut ties with them was the best way I could love and care for myself.

Though I played an important role in caring for my siblings. They are no longer my job or responsibility. They are God's. Trying to make those relationships whole and happy is out of the parameters of my job description and superhero powers.

Letting them go was the best gift I ever gave myself. It freed my soul. It liberated my heart.

I am the absolute "last" person my family would look to, as an example of a Christian they should emulate. There is too much dysfunctional history, programming, and distrust to follow my advice or actions. God has them and knows what they need and who to use in order to get their attention.

I'm seen exactly as I am by my family. A hypocrite and sinner who they have an unfortunate past with. These are the very excuses many people use to stay away from Christians and the church. That is the enemy's plan to keep people away from Christ. My belief and desire to be with God has everything to do with the fact I am an unlovable, undeserving sinner. In no way do I view myself as better than someone who doesn't follow the Lord. I just happen to see myself as loved and forgiven.

I love each of my family members and continue to pray fervently for them. Prayer is not a last resort. It's the first line of defense. I meet with God on their behalf daily. I choose to not be in relationships with them as they are toxic and that is what I work terribly hard at untangling myself from. Given the opportunity or occasion to be around them, the same dysfunctional interplay erupts. It's as if we're on autopilot. Unhealthy and toxic behaviors occur, that are long ingrained in our brains. For this reason, we must stay apart.

I'm fully confident that God is on the job and hears my prayers. I have nothing to prove about being smart. I'm technically just trying to drown out the voices in my head from those who contributed to the distorted picture that lives and lies inside my head.

As a rule, when I'm consistently ruminating on a subject or bringing it up repeatedly, I'm likely trying to resolve it in my head. It is never helpful to tell me to, just let it go. It is worse to blame and shame me into believing I have the power to let go of my past and stuff it away as if it never occurred. It seems to others that every time I bring up something from my childhood, that's evidence that I won't let go of it. The truth is, that recollecting my past is a reminder of being rescued and loved by God.

It's astounding to me that so many people who feel qualified to psychologically counsel me, in truth have horribly and dangerously missed the mark. Trauma and abuse do not ever go away. At best, we can learn important coping strategies and ways to accept to a point the atrocities done to us. Our bodies carry the brunt and burden of our abuse. We do not possess the power to heal ourselves but can most assuredly fool ourselves into believing we can.

This kind of strategy falls into the same situation of blaming me for my illnesses and diseases. I've had well-meaning Christians set me down and explain to me that the reason I have sickness is due to my lack of faith.

This is not only Biblically incorrect because Faith is God-given and I can't manufacture it myself, but again blaming the victim. I've also been told that when I have a problem, it's because I'm not in God's Word enough. Are there secret Word monitors I'm not aware of? The notion is ludicrous and again puts the burden and blame squarely onto the victim.

I am not just book smart, I'm people smart. That is more valuable to me than being able to quote Shakespeare. It is also more intimidating to some. People can get nervous around someone who can read them accurately and can't be fooled. It leaves them feeling unsure and exposed. People have ended relationships with me over this. I lost a job once over this. It is what ultimately got me thrown out of my parents' house. I can't help but I'm gifted with insight that others might not possess. It has been invaluable to me and as an older adult, I heavily rely on it to include or exclude people in my world.

Do not let your difficulties convince you that you're not smart. Do not allow the bad days you experience to confuse you into thinking you have a bad life. God is always in control. Always.

I'm learning to abide in Christ. Abiding in Him is the difference between an intimate close relationship versus a superficial acquaintance.

In the grand scheme of things, being smart might not seem like such an important issue. To the trauma victim who grew up feeling stupid in every way, a glimmer of brightness that looks like wisdom or "smarts," means everything. Feeling not so dumb is healing to your soul.

I regularly have conversations with myself, assuring "me" that I'm OK, I'm not stupid, not perfect but I am smart and intuitive. I am giving myself ongoing pep talks a lot. It's another way to drown out the negative voices from my childhood that swim around in my brain, attempting to convince me I'm helpless and worthless and should not be here.

Proverbs 4:6-7
Do not forsake wisdom, and she will watch over you. Wisdom is supreme; therefore, get wisdom. Though it costs all you have, get an understanding.

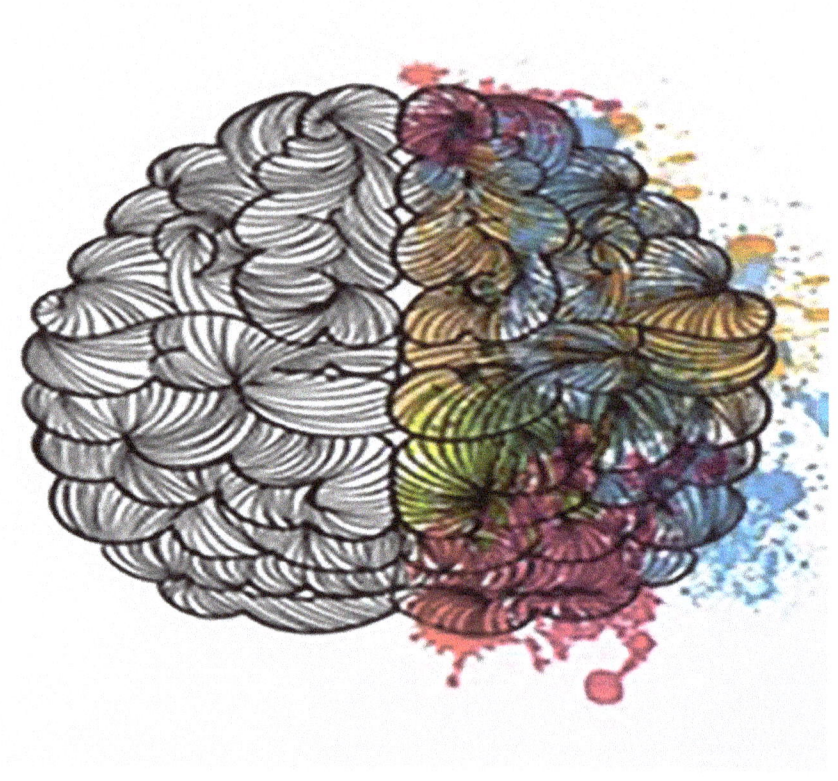

BIOLOGY ISN'T EVERYTHING

Your family isn't everything. If your family is actually a threat to your psychological well-being, it's not important to keep up the façade that they are everything. Your emotional and mental health along with the relationship you have with yourself, and God is everything. Abusive family dynamics should be eliminated from the equation. Free yourself from the bondage of your dangerous biological family if need be.

We each have the life we are willing to tolerate. If you want more from life, expect more from yourself and those around you. Don't continue to shrink yourself to fit into spaces you've long outgrown or no longer belong.

The importance of setting yourself free from your toxic dysfunctional family dynamics is the only way to begin the process of healing. Stepping back into those relationships only serves to revive and continue repeating the same emotional destruction you grew up in. When you do break free it's perfectly normal to feel relief along with some grief. It's OK to love people and still keep your distance from them.

If you do not attempt to address and work through your childhood trauma, your adult relationships will.

When you give up on someone, it doesn't necessarily mean that you don't care, even though others might see it that way. What it generally signals is, that you have finally realized that they are the ones who don't care. Staying in one-sided relationships is harming you. You deserve the same respect, attention, and loyalty you give. You learned to expect less because so little was invested in you as a child. It's not important how much effort you expend. It will never make up for someone else's lack of effort. Other people's actions will tell the story of how they feel about you. Never listen to a person's words about how they feel. Rely on what they do and show you through actions.

Whatever took place in your family horror show was not your fault. You did not deserve the abuses you had to endure. Nothing was ever your fault. Unfortunately, you are the one left trying to figure out your childhood wounds, taking responsibility for understanding, unlearning, and restoring all the responses and reactions that have been conditioned into your nervous system by those who failed you as a child. If you're angry about that, it's perfectly acceptable.

Choose to be proud of yourself for walking away from people who repeatedly treated you badly. That is an adult response to childhood abuse. If you choose to wait until others act correctly, you are disrespecting yourself. You are compromising your self- worth for someone who does not know or respect your values.

The definition of family was not meant to include these dysfunctional behaviors like keeping secrets and lies sacred or always having to walk on eggshells. It also doesn't mean lying to keep the peace and pretending everyone is mentally healthy when they aren't. It doesn't mean tiptoeing around the truth and avoiding being real. It never means tolerating and defending abusive behavior. Pretending everything is fine when it isn't, covering up secrets and lies, and denying substance abuse.

In my family, every one of these rules or guidelines was violated. The most egregious violation was being sworn to secrecy about everything that happened in our home. Boundaries are very difficult to set when you have lived your life in fear. That if you upset anyone, the response would be immediate anger and they would turn on you or completely reject you.

My mother's favorite phrase was "shame on you." She used it to bully everyone into submission. It worked well because most of the time she got her way. I recall a holiday visit to my family's home on Thanksgiving. I was only going to be there for a few short days. It had been a twenty-four-hour drive to get there. We were exhausted from driving straight through and hoped for some much-needed relaxation visiting with my family.

My mother had come up with many ways to use my services and skills while there, but truthfully, I did not care to take on any of my mother's chores, errands, or projects. I had not been there long when she handed me a pile of note cards and a box of cut-out recipes. She asked me to type all her recipes onto the index cards. This was nothing I cared to do; however, you just don't say no to my mother.

I allowed myself to feel all the feelings attached to my mother's demands. I call them demands because it was expected that you do as you told. For the first time, I told her NO. My reason for saying no to her was that I didn't want to do it, plain and simple. Her immediate reaction was to tell me "Shame on me," and next, how "mean and selfish" I was.

She was right about my being selfish. I was determined to do so. I was not going to cave into her shame and criticism. I got my power back. I did not let her verbal assault change my mind. I had won, but the win came at a cost. She gave me the silent treatment for about a year.

James 4:17
So whoever knows the right thing to do and fails to do it, for him it is a sin.

THE GOOD FIGHT

I'm incredibly smart (clever genius) and do not take criticism well. That does not mean I can't admit when I'm wrong, it simply means if I'm criticized it might be kinder to just shoot me dead. A monumental pain wrapped in self-defeat eats at the very core of my being. That very criticism, large or small, is all the evidence required to condemn my existence. Criticism isn't about getting something wrong; it speaks to my incompetence, foolishness, and lack of self-worth.

It hurts because I've generally explored everything thoroughly that comes out of my mouth. I do so to not be wrong. I'm not prone to opinions or information that I've not thoroughly researched. I never want to look stupid. I work hard as a student of life to be well-rehearsed and knowledgeable on important topics.

It's not that there is something wrong with being wrong, it's that in my brain the only noise I hear during a criticism, is run, hide, isolate, and out of that comes self-loathing and condemnation.

One of my worst triggers is looking stupid. I was made to feel that way growing up but in actuality, I'm the smartest in my family. I secretly believed I was all alone. To prove it, I purchased I.Q. tests that we all took together. I scored the highest. I wasn't just a clever genius; I truly am a genius.

Armed with proof of my intelligence has not made me feel more secure. I still live with the feelings of stupidity and my aunt frequently describes me as the smartest dumb person she knows. Yes, that is abusive, especially in light of my insecurity about that.

I realize no one in my family will ever admit that I know anything or have any special knowledge of something. It goes against their narrative. They would have to change and that my friends, is a dirty word in our family. Truthfully, I believe I'm scared of my family. I'm cut from the same cloth but not at all the same patterns. I'm open to change and self-evaluation. I want my life to be different and God-centered. I actively work on my problems. This does not make me perfect or better than others, it makes me different. It means I'm in love with my Savior.

In that, I can be seen as threatening to my family. It used to hurt me deeply that I was not respected for being who I am. Now I don't care. I stopped beating my head against the proverbial brick wall, in favor of choosing to love and accepting myself as I am. I don't need validation from my dysfunctional family to be well. Deciding to cut ties with them was the best way I could love and care for myself.

My siblings are no longer my job or responsibility. They are God's. Trying to make those relationships whole and happy is out of the parameters of my job description and superhero powers. Letting them go was the best gift I ever gave myself. It freed my soul.

You see, I've recently learned a valuable lesson regarding rejection. People who don't return a call or offer an explanation regarding rude behavior are dishonest and passive-aggressive, it's not because of you, it's because those are not people for you. You will never be right for the wrong person. There is no need to feel the rejection of someone who's not there to step up to the bar for you. Get rid of them fast.

Make room for the right people God will send your way. It's perfectly correct to love them all and continue to pray fervently for them. Prayer is not a last resort. It's the first line of defense. I meet with God on their behalf daily.

They are no longer active participants in your world because they aren't for you, but you choose to honor them just the same.

1 Thessalonians 5:12-13
Now we ask you, brothers, to respect those who work hard among you and are over you in the Lord and who admonish you, hold them in the highest regard in love because of their work. Live in peace with one another.

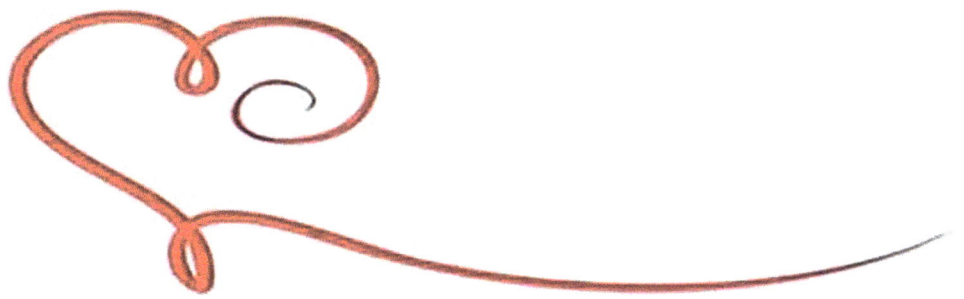

REASONS WHY

There are always good, solid, logical, and acceptable reasons why crap happens. We cling to those reasons as justification for our responses. The truth is those reasons are reasons only. They are not good excuses for bad behavior. They are excuses, just not good ones. We can always muster up a plausible excuse. We can even make it sound justifiable. There is never only one response to anything. Reasons can also be feelings and feelings can often be based on faulty thinking. We cannot always count on our emotional responses to be legitimate. We also have to factor in unemotional facts. There are choices to be made about the direction one wishes to go in life. Choose wisely and soberly.

It's easy to hide behind our circumstances as victims. It grants us sympathy and we can hold people hostage to gift us special mercy and compassion. We are, after all, victims. We did not ask for trauma and chaos; it sought us out.

Getting past being a victim and committing oneself to change is a big decision that sometimes seems impossible. God does not leave us alone in that endeavor. He is paving the way ahead of us, blessing the journey with every step forward.

Make no mistake, it is hard work. It's a process and everyone's walk is different. There is no room for comparison. It is wonderful to grant support and prayer to these brave souls. Kind words and validation are so helpful.

Satan is working hard to derail the process. He doesn't want healing for any of God's children. If we stay broken, we are also staying in bondage with evil. The cycle of victimization carries on. We continue to hurt ourselves and those around us. Hurt people, hurt others.

Be brave. Let God be the Hero in your story. His love never abandons us. Clutching onto the reasons why we are victims only serves to keep us down in the pit of darkness. God wants us to function as His beloved children. He wants us to believe, and trust in His love.

1 John 3:1
See what kind of love the Father has given to us, that we should be called children of God, and so we are. The reason why the world does not know us is that it did not know Him.

WHAT I WANT TO BE WHEN I GROW UP!

I do not want to die the poster child for trauma and abuse. I further resent the term "survivor" also. It implies I saved myself from something. I had nothing to do with surviving. That was God's plan for me. My abusers just weren't proficient enough at ending my life. The perpetrator's plans for me didn't align with God's plan for my life.

I care about people deeply and with and with deliberate intention. However, all my life I thought that was the definition of love. It has been more challenging to care for myself and with the same intent, feed and nurture my soul.

I derived my self-worth from having very few needs of my own and meeting everyone else's needs. It's what I strove for. There was no one in my corner caring for me.

I'm the classic co-dependent. I'm well trained like a circus animal. I'm quite mailable and impressionable. I'm an easy mark. People see me coming. I'm certain a sign exits on me that everyone but me can see, saying "victim."

It's quite difficult for me to look introspectively inside my persona and determine who I am. No longer content to sit on the sidelines waiting for the forgotten or forbidden invitation. "I" am starting to show up at the party, and I'm looking for fun.

Glimpses of who I am and who I'm choosing to be are beginning to poke through the hard surface of an identity that isn't my own. It was an identity created out of fear, sadness, and an effort to protect myself at all costs from possible death.

Those self-preservation maneuvers have cost me dearly. They are not user-friendly. I've lost friendships, family, and the essence of who I am. Now I'm working to destroy that which has sought to destroy me and my happiness, sanity, and every breath I take over the span of a lifetime.

Much of my life was squandered away because of what others had done to me. Not because I'm not intelligent but because I bought the lie that I wasn't. Trauma and abuse stole my ability and desire to move forward. I became insecure and was not confident in my abilities to achieve anything worthwhile. My sexual abuse caused a tragic academic collapse in my future. Another natural consequence of being raised in an environment where your developmental needs are denied, ignored, or mocked.

This is fairly typical behavior for a child victim of sex abuse and should have been a red flag for my educators. The abuse certainly affected my self-confidence, but we also moved a lot which didn't help much with my scholarly motivation. There was little educational stability or continuity. That mirrored my home life to a tree.

I often wonder who I could have been had I not had all the heavy insecurities that plagued me. All caused by trauma and abuse. It makes me sad, and I feel cheated out of a more fulfilling life. I grieve this as a genuine and regrettable loss.

Our family moved 9 times in 18 years. We changed states 5 times. There was a significant reason for these moves. We were not in the military as I was often asked. We were running. Sex offenders frequently run.

As a young student, changing schools was troublesome. I was never asked if I had homework. No interest was paid to any schoolwork brought home. No one ever asked about my day or inquired about what I liked or disliked. I think school was treated more as a babysitter, so my mom could have a break from so many children.

Curiously, my report cards were saved along with one piece of artwork. It was a card made for my abusive, sexually inappropriate, gay stepfather. It said, "To Daddy my favorite Planet."

I could try to psychoanalyze this till Jesus called me home, but that small child was somehow trying to make peace with her tormentor. The card survived and lived amongst thousands of papers carted home by six children over 30 years. Why this artifact? It honestly brings me to tears. I don't want it but can't seem to let it go. It is a small cry and longing for hope. It is, after all, me.

This instability and constant movement created barriers that made academic success a hardship to endure and overcome. I was a traumatized child, being further traumatized by the uncertainty of where I would be living. Who my teacher would be and who if anyone cared.

How does a child rise above instead of falling in those conditions? I dropped out of college three times. Each time it devastated my heart and spoke to me in the language of failure. A language I was fluent in.

None of us children adapted well to the constant moves. I probably adjusted the best. For me, a move meant a new beginning which in turn led to a small measure of hope that I might be recognized as someone good instead of someone bad. It was also an opportunity to leave the clutches of whoever the current predators were.

Each of the children in our house has multiple psychiatric, social, substance abuse, and food issues. We are not close at all. That was part of my mother's design for each of us. If we did not interact or were not close, then we would not be prone to collectively unravel the proverbial twisted yarn ball. To not look too hard or question the sanity of our upbringing and existence.

My mother's strategy worked for most of us. Of the six of us who grew up together, I'm the oldest. I'm the most psychologically inquisitive and committed to lifelong learning. This combination made me a threat and always did in my parents' eyes. I was driven to the nearest freeway and told to leave town and never return at age 17.

My sister Debbie did not question anything, but I don't know an angrier human on the planet. She gets physically violent. She even struck an employee once. I bear the scars of her anger. Hence, living in a basement was far safer than sharing a room with her. Her rages are legendary, and she has been banned from businesses and restaurants for them.

My brother Philip, I pray his soul is at rest and peace, set three fires in our home as a child and routinely ran away. This caused my mother to tie him with a rope to our kitchen. He could only go as far as the bathroom. He unfortunately was beaten daily by my stepfather's belt upon his arrival home from work and was also molested by my stepfather. He was a pathological liar who led an entirely secret life that wasn't discovered until his death. We do not have any idea who Philip's father is. That secret went to the grave with everyone who knew the truth.

My sister Cathy is our only lifetime alcoholic, who followed in her parents' footsteps. We were all substance abusers, but she found a true friend and comfort in alcohol. She's an enigma. She's quiet until she opens her gutter mouth. She slept with family members and anyone else she could find. This type of promiscuity is a trauma response. I don't judge her mistakes; I don't deny or hide the behaviors either.

I keep track of her and her family by googling her city and state arrest records. There I found them on the internet as their arrest warrants lead. The sadness and sorrow ooze onto everyone.

My sister Claire is another truth seeker, and she wants dates, names, places, and court documents. She's the official family historian and keeper of the paper trail. She has spent much of her lifetime living in her car, by choice. She does not interact or play nicely with others. She is prone to tantrums and bouts of paranoia. She isolates more than any of us. She will not speak to you for twenty years and call you on the phone and talk as if time stood still.

I love her the most and fear her the most. Her unpredictability and anger scare me. She's a lesbian (dyke) who isn't at all sure about me being a Christian. Claire was also booted from our house at age 17. My mother packed a suitcase for her before opening the front door for her to leave. She lived in the local park so she could finish high school and graduate. Friends fed er and she bathed at a local gas station.

My brother Michael is my mother's baby and the worst victim. He has no memory of his childhood at all. He does not have friends. He is married, not divorced, yet. He has three daughters and that is his life. He's been academically successful and has a successful career. He is also a substance abuser. He was a big drug dealer in high school. He frequently had drugs delivered to my parent's house and my mother unknowingly signed for them C.O.D.

My mother was sexually enmeshed with him and my stepfather was enmeshed with me. His first outward act of defiance towards my mother was leaving the state to go to college and staying with long-time family friends. He had an affair with our friend's wife. He was signaling to my mother that she had been replaced. He was very angry. Our dear longtime family friend will have nothing to do with our family now. He was unfairly ensnared in our unholy drama. You might wonder where

God fits into our family unit. God was a sporadic fixture. We brought Him out on Christmas and Easter. He, however, never left our side. He heard my cries for love and happiness. He heard our sorrow, yet I'm the only one who believed and clung to Him. He sought us all.

Me before the world stole my childhood.

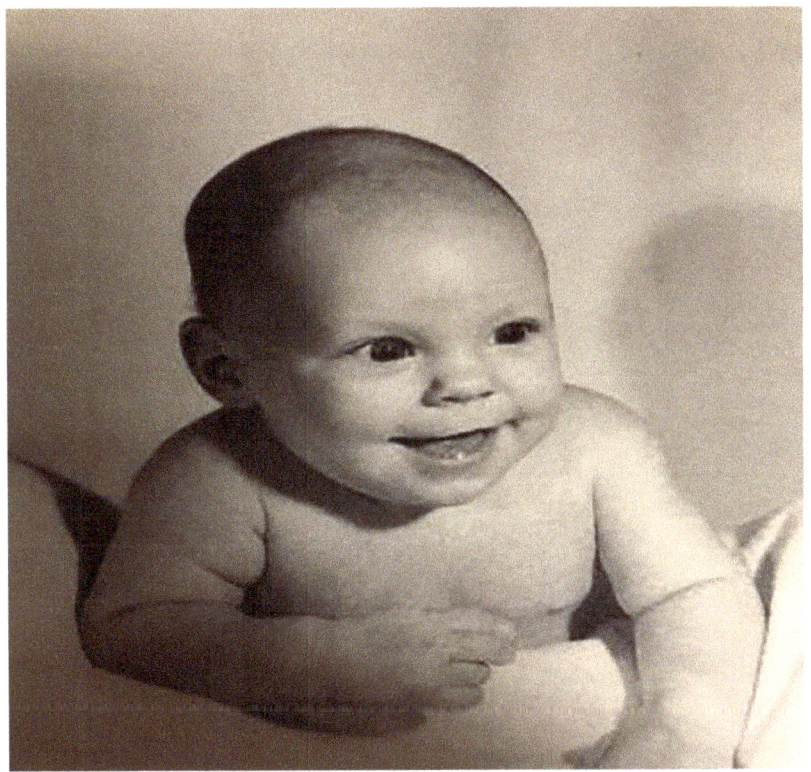

LAUGH LOTS

Have you ever laughed so hard and so long that you start to snort and cry a little? Then no sound emanates from you at all and you become unable to breathe and lastly, you pee your pants? My daughters and I had many episodes of drunken laughter like this. It's satisfying and fun and you just want it to stop all at the same time.

I can find humor in just about anything. The reason for this is quite literally, survival. It also holds my interest, entertains me, and lets me know how clever and quick-witted I am. My sister Claire is the funniest in my family and could even make my mother laugh. A genuine accomplishment worth bragging about. It was rare when she laughed but an event worth noting when it occurred.

If I can make people laugh, it takes the bright spotlight off of my true emotions. It's how I avoid social isolation and all manners of discrimination related to prejudice about my mental health issues too.

I'm at my best when being funny, playing with others, and just having fun, I don't have to explain, convince, or justify my feelings for the billionth time. Don't be fooled though. Behind the laughter is a crap storm of pain and suffering. I believe this to be true for many creative people. There is much sadness behind the façade of laughter in the artistic mind. Creativity is camouflage for the broken soul.

The personalities of creatives are more fluid along with being more rebellious. These traits can cause creative individuals' feelings of depression or social alienation. Those people who are less creative respond to situations according to what they have been told by those in authority. They are less likely to question the status quo. It is also difficult for the creative mind to accept compliments, as they are more apt to agree with their critics.

This explains a lot about who I am and how I perceive myself. It doesn't matter if you tell me how good I am, it's not going to register. That inability to honestly assess one's genuine strengths never stops a creative from continuing to be creative. There has not been a creative stone unturned, that I have not engaged in or explored. I'm driven by the need to create, be it art, poetry, design, music, quilting, or working to make people laugh.

When I'm making you laugh, I'm also humoring myself. I am, after all, a clever genius. I love a good laugh. If you're funny, I'll follow you anywhere. The first law of attraction for me is humor. It is not always a good test or measure for a partner though. Funny doesn't always equal good dating or marriage material, as I've learned the hard way. Being funny has become my "red flag" for a potential love interest.

That is why I took myself out of the relationship game altogether. I'm a very bad picker. I should be alone then continuing to end up in ridiculously painful, destructive relationships. I'm good being alone.

Along with laughter being a survival skill, so is my sarcasm. With my quick wit, sarcasm Is where I outshine my entire family. Claire was the master at humor. I'm the master of sarcasm. Not the kind of sarcasm designed to injure others, but the humorous kind.

I have numerous serious health conditions. I laugh hysterically every time I get a new health diagnosis. REALLY!!! SERIOUSLY!!! HONESTLY!!!

Not only is it humorous to me but it's phenomenal. I get things no one has ever heard of. This fascinates me. I'm not sure why Satan bothers with me. My faith is unshakable. To keep giving me more and rare conditions seems like overkill. I take it in stride because I've learned to accept and even embrace my ongoing health trials. Not much gets me down or stops me.

Don't forget to have fun along the way. This world can be hilarious even in the face of tragedy, if you allow yourself to see it. I'm not diminishing the reality of my maladies or anyone else's, just having fun with them. If I don't, I'll never get out of bed or stop crying in my cereal. I refuse to live like I'm dying.

I've been known to put a routine together and go to our local comedy club and perform. Once they were doing auditions there for a new television sitcom and I attended the audition. We were each filmed for the television show. I am extremely out of my comfort zone doing this, but it's also a fundamental need I have. A need for humor, to be funny and make people laugh.

I need humorous and intelligent people who can intellectually, psychologically, and humorously spar with me. My physical therapist Chris is quite proficient at this. We can play together easily and are both creative geniuses. I'm never more in my element and ready to "play," than when I'm at physical therapy.

God has blessed me with Chris and his gift of complex intelligent humor and caring nature. God knows my need for giving, caring unshakable and compassionate souls. He never fails to place the right people at the right time in my path, to squarely fit my need. God knows me better than I know myself.

Be funny. Find funny people who get you to play with. It helps take the sting out of life. Try and find humor in every stressful, asking, unfair, hurtful, and anxiety-ridden situation. You will gain nuggets of joy along the way.

Puerto Rico 1978

REASONS WHY

There are always good, solid, logical, and acceptable reasons why crap happens in life. We cling to those reasons as justification for how we feel along with our symptoms and responses. The truth is those reasons are just reasons only. Reasons why bad things happen are not good excuses for responding with more bad behavior. They are in fact "excuses," but they are not accurate or good ones. We can always muster up a plausible excuse. We can even make it sound justifiable in our minds.

We can pick apart behavior and try to understand the abuses left by those who traumatize, murder, and torture. It's much like the FAA, which spends endless hours and work recreating a plane crash piece by piece trying to determine the cause of that disaster. It can be done but no matter how much technical knowledge and information is discovered it never changes the outcome.

After becoming a victim, there are choices to be made about the direction one wishes to go in life. You can remain a victim and become helpless or rise above and become resilient and strong. No matter how hard it is to heal from trauma, it's ultimately much harder to stay stuck in the victim role. Without you even realizing it, your body will begin to react negatively to your grief and sadness. Then it will become your "job" to manage doctors and appointments. It's extremely tiring and time-consuming.

It's easy to hide behind our circumstances and what we were left powerless to change as victims. We can feel sorry for ourselves and it's not difficult to get others to do the same. In a certain way, self-pity allows for the opportunity to hold people hostage to feeling bad and sympathetic to our pain. We have an overabundance of pain. We are, after all, victims. We did not ask for trauma, abuse, and chaos but it came to us anyway.

Getting past being a victim and committing oneself to change is a big decision that sometimes seems impossible. God does not leave us alone to work it out for ourselves. He is clearing the way ahead of us, blessing the journey, and quieting us with every step forward.

Make no mistake, it is hard work. It may require the rest of your life, to work at healing. It's a process and everyone's walk is different. There is no room for comparison. There is no possible way to achieve total healing and wellness as a victim. Things can often improve. Strategies for coping in healthier ways help to improve our daily living. It is worth the pain to work on healing.

While actively working on the healing process you will find moments where mental fortitude is required. Your strength of will can be challenged. The entire process moves into a full- body experience, and it will become exhausting. You can't underestimate Satan's attempts to derail the process.

Being connected and aware does not come easily to childhood abuse survivors. Learning new ways of behaving intentionally and seeking to find and appreciate happiness is a total-body experience. Some days will require us to be well-rested. Make time for it because that too is an essential element of healing.

Through healing, things can be better with God's help. That it is He, who is our refuge and strength and is the true healing we seek and need.

It is wonderful to grant support and prayer to the brave souls seeking refuge, strength, and hope in Christ. They are with God's Mercy and Grace, able to cling to Christ in their pain. A kind word and validation are so helpful to those wrestling with these mountainous challenges.

Satan is working hard to keep us endlessly adrift and continually in doubt. He creates shaky hands and unsteady feet. He doesn't want healing for any of God's children. Satan will talk you out of God's love with his lies. Satan knows scripture in its entirety and will attempt to confuse us with it. Satan wants us to stay broken, because then we are also staying in bondage with evil. The cycle of victimization carries on. We continue to hurt ourselves and those around us.

Be brave. Let God be the hero in your story. His love never abandons us. Holding on tightly to the reasons why we are victims only serves to keep us down in the pit of darkness. God wants us to function as His beloved children and servants. He longs to help us become free from our burdens. He also wants us to believe, and trust in His love. It is very real and substantial.

God is sufficient and generous to supply a place of healing and respite for all of us in all our needs. His goal is to bind our wounds and take the weight of our trauma from us. We have a good God like that.

2 Corinthians 12:9
But He said to me, my grace is sufficient for you, for my power is made perfect in weakness. Therefore, I will boast all the more gladly about my weaknesses, so that Christ's power may rest on me.

Psalm 126: Then our mouth was filled with laughter and our tongue with shouts of joy; then they said among the nations, "The Lord has done great things for them."

A FAMILY OF MY OWN

I have always wanted to be a mom. Subconsciously I wished to atone for the two children I lost. One to abortion and one to miscarriage soon after the abortion. Consciously I was determined to have someone to love.

I wanted my children to love me back but did not assume they would. A fear I experienced at the birth of my oldest daughter. I was going to have to parent and fight against all my insecurities and deficits, with only the blueprint I had. That could never work. I understood what "not" to do but had no reasonable experience as to "what" to do.

The most blessed days I ever had and by far my happiest were the births of my children.

I was never in more pain and had almost died during one birth and had anesthesia accidents during both births. It didn't matter because I had my girls.

The joy I had in my heart was actively competing with my fear of failure as a parent. I was painfully aware of my inadequate preparedness to be a great mom. It didn't matter how hard I might work at it or want it; I was going to get it wrong because of my horrid background. I don't possess supernatural powers. I'm good at lots of things but changing a lifetime of abuse responses and behaviors was beyond my skill set.

I was a very protective parent. I did not trust anyone with my children. That was my reaction to my childhood trauma.

My husband had beat me in the middle of the night while I was asleep when I was eight and a half months pregnant. I woke up with him punching me in my stomach as hard as possible. He was trying to kill my baby and quite possibly me too. I screamed at him to stop and asked him what he was doing.

When he finally stopped pounding on my stomach, I asked him what he was doing. He said he must have been having a bad dream. It was an unconvincing story. We never discussed it again. We both knew the truth.

A few days later, my daughter was born via C-section. Her eyes were swollen. Her forehead was black and blue and her cheek had a deep red mark.

She should not have had a mark on her. She did not go through the birth canal. She had been injured by her father during that beating.

I stayed in denial about the reality of what had happened. It was easier to believe my husband that while having a nightmare he attacked me in his sleep. Even in my denial, I knew I could never trust him with my child. Ever!

My favorite photo, Puerto Rico 1979

A NEW SONG

I'm no longer embracing the shreds of my life like a warm fuzzy kitten, stroking its back into submission. Or trying to tame it by hugging it harder. I'm getting a dog!

The education I received in life's academy (or growing up Zissis) was how to continue the unhealthy cycle of abuse where everyone else left off. I was an amazing student and learned helplessness and self-destruction well. I was proficient enough to tutor myself in additional ways of self-annihilation. No doubt my inspiration came from well-honed abuse tactics.

It was not just me who suffered. I unconsciously but frequently bled my sadness onto my children. My love did not conquer all. It did not ease the hemorrhaging at the time.

Love is going to ultimately win in the end. GOD is and always has been in control. His love never fails.

God has heard my cries and is faithfully acknowledging and addressing my pain and sorrow. He is speaking to me loud and clear, "NO MORE."

My ultimate job is to listen and obey. I began this journey to wellness in earnest almost three years ago after a most determined suicide attempt. Then at His prompting a little over a year ago, I started writing daily devotionals feverishly. The more I wrote the thirstier I became. I had discovered the fountain of life. The Living Water. God was transforming me and I was surrendering to His will. I was firmly in His grasp.

Along the way, I lost more and more people in my life. Not randomly but with precision as if God was cutting with a razor. He was eliminating all the emotionally dangerous people, the one-sided relationships, and lastly my children. Potential trauma triggers were lessened. One cannot heal visiting with your co-trauma survivors, gravitating back to the fire. That is another way of just coping and surviving, not healing.

This is especially true when it is only you on a healing path in your family. You become a target. The designated patient. The one they'll point to you as crazy and the problem source. It is tremendously important to get free from that dynamic.

Losing my children has not been pleasant but I have peace and calm about it and a resolution that this too is part of God's plan. I've not only surrendered myself to God but surrendered my children to Him. They are His and not mine to dysfunctional cling to. My children are not my lifeline, He is. He cares for them equally and is a far better parent.

So, what am I left with? Certainly, with growing pains. Excited for the future and not the least bit worried. God's peace that passes all understanding whispers to me.

Joy and gratitude are new emotions I'm grappling with. Sometimes it feels like touching a hot stove. I inclined to just not do it. God is asking me to place my trust in Him. I'm leaving the battle of who is sitting on the throne to Him. That throne was custom-built for Him. I don't belong in it. My place is beside Him.

God is deeply embedded in my heart. I no longer question His love for me. I'm excited for all that is to come.

My ultimate goal in getting my head well is to die with an understanding of happiness. I did not want to die lost, sad, and feeling all alone in a crowded room. I want my children to respect my efforts and choice to begin a healing journey in earnest, not just the mouthing of empty words and promises. A legacy of worth. They may never have an opportunity to witness the transformation in my life, but will have an opportunity if they choose, to read about it.

God got this! He speaks to me and assures me a transformational destination awaits. He is driving the bus. I'm buckled in tight. I've got the binoculars He's provided.

My life is full of miracles. We don't always get to see them. God has also provided a plan for me that He alone watered and grew, allowing me to witness the fruit. We do not always get that glimpse either. I'm so grateful for His presence, intense hand-holding, guidance, and detour signs posted along the way.

My soul rejoices and sings His praise!

THANKSGIVING, THANKSGIVINGS

I'm 68 years old and have been present at many Thanksgivings. At our house, my mother would do the cooking and my stepfather carved the bird. Mom would trot out the "good" gas station dishes and good silverware. I was never certain how the day would turn out, but it always began with lots of wine and cigarettes and ended pretty much the same way. It was a day I had a definite love/hate relationship with. I wanted to be a part of it because that's what families do. I wanted to avoid it too, in favor of peace.

My mother would make everyone's favorite dessert except mine. That meant a cherry pie, cherry cream cheese pie, lemon meringue pie, and pumpkin pie were present. My favorite pie was pecan. It was never made until I started making it myself.

Dinner could be a crap shoot. There was no telling how the food would turn out. We regularly "rated" the meal. We recounted past Thanksgiving cooking disasters every year. We remember and speak up about these cooking errors but never mention why they occurred. Our parents were drunk.

We were even served mashed potato soup once. Too much milk went in because too much alcohol was drunk by my mother. We recount that story annually but avoid the obvious reason it happened.

In actuality, we were forbidden by my stepfather to ever mention my mother's drunken behavior. We'd been properly warned.

We did not as a rule have guests for our feast. When and if we did, it was a bigger, more noticeable disaster. Our embarrassment for everyone present was palpable. Silence ensued. It wrecked our vibe. It challenged our sensibilities. It noticed the elephant in the room. It silently shamed us with our reality. It was the mirror we always avoided looking into. Who wants that on a major holiday that celebrates things to be thankful for? We clung tightly to our denial, especially on special occasions.

If having a guest made us uncomfortable, imagine how any guests felt. I had a boyfriend once. It is now a family story legend are made of. Certifiable folklore. The story of that dysfunctional event was told over and over every following Thanksgiving. I would never live it down and the retelling of the tale was not just a reminder of the boundary I crossed but was also my punishment. How dare I bring a guest!

I invited a girlfriend over once, just to witness the circus event. I had explained to her what would take place from the minute the front door opened, play-by-play. I did not disappoint her. Thanksgiving had now become a spectator sport for those brave enough to attend and witness the carnage. To be present at our table, one had to endure coldness, uncomfortable stares, and the notion they'd intruded on a private nightmare. They would never feel welcome.

While Thanksgiving is a special day for most, it was more of a dysfunctional instant replay of a liquor-fueled endurance event (that just happened to involve an innocent turkey) for our family. We overstuffed ourselves to the point of pain and laid around like beached whales groaning for relief, hours afterward.

My mother rarely sat at the table with us, as she preferred to be "serving" us. She would be tripping over furniture and manhandling my baby brother. When she had at least half a box of wine on board, it was impossible to keep her hands off my brother. She smothered him with pats and paws. Stroked his head and nuzzled him into her chest. It was an uncomfortable display to witness. I ached for him. It was never going to turn out good.

I've often been the guest at friends' homes for Thanksgiving now that I am not inclined to cook such a large meal for one. Most of the time it is very enjoyable. I've only had one excruciatingly bad experience at someone's house.

I was invited to a Thanksgiving meal at a friend's I know from church. They had a six-year-old daughter who taught me a new game I'd never played before. I thoroughly enjoyed it. That was the only highlight. The entire rest of the visit was listening to constant bickering, backbiting, insulting, passive-aggressive, and aggressive behaviors. I wanted to slither away quietly. I was astonished by this display. Even my dysfunctional family understood how to play nice when witnesses were present. It's as if I weren't there observing the chaos and noticing the wincing faces their daughter made and her attempts at attention to deflect the fray. This was painful for her and yet probably very typical. Thanksgiving isn't wonderful all the time for everyone.

I've properly set the stage for Thanksgiving 2021. I was invited to spend the day with my boss's tribe. I was happy for the invitation. I was not certain however that I would attend. It seemed like the perfect opportunity to get some additional sleep and tackle cleaning I'd been unable to accomplish due to my busy schedule.

My other excuse was I'd applied more purple semi-permanent hair color on my head and left it in too long. It was much more intense than usual. I felt like a nightmare participant in the wrong holiday. I was fine for Easter but not so much for Thanksgiving. I tried washing my hair about 10 times. My hair wasn't giving up the neon purple.

At the last minute, I decided to go, deep pinkish purple hair or not. I'd just avoid mirrors. What you can't see, can't hurt you, or in my situation, scare and embarrass me.

I bought a large pumpkin pie and brought flowers for my host and went to "hopefully" enjoy my day.

It was a great crowd in a spacious home. Everyone was exceptionally friendly and smart, with the proper amount of humorous (not dangerous) sarcasm.

I'm a talker and storyteller who loves intelligent conversations. This was a crowd I could spar with and match wits with effortlessly.

When it came time to eat, we thanked the Good Lord for His many blessings and offered Him additional petitions on behalf of those who were ill. We let the children hit the food line first, avoiding their difficulty waiting and the ability to complain without ceasing. It was an excellent call.

As I filled my plate with all things scrumptious and found a suitable place to sit, I began the most divine Thanksgiving dinner I ever ate.

The day was perfect. It was effortless for me to navigate socially and emotionally. I can say it was joyous and satisfying. I left astounded remembering all the Thanksgiving days of my past and the sadness of them. Then I realized I'd had the most perfect Thanksgiving ever.

This was what fellowship in the Lord was like. This was the richness of His blessings poured down from Heaven. This was not only amazing food for the stomach but nourishment for the soul. Not that I hadn't had similar times with my Christian family before, but this was special and different. I'm convinced my healing heart played a part in being able to notice and receive the experience in a way I was unable to in the past.

One could not possibly leave hungry from that day and instead could only leave satisfied and content. Stomach and heart well fed. I waited 68 years for an experience I didn't even recognize my hunger for.

God has worked hard in my life to help me receive His gifts without the idea of "strings attached" to everything good. Gone was me waiting for the other proverbial shoe to drop.

God never disappoints! I praise Him endlessly. He is Good and devoted to lifting us above our pain and struggles. Thanksgiving blessed!

ME NEGATIVE?

I am frequently accused of being negative. That is actually not true. What I am is a chronic venter. I vent as a result of any negativity I encounter in my day. I do this to get rid of it. To hear the event out loud. And to gain insight or mostly agreement that I had been wronged or otherwise placed in a difficult situation. I want validation. It's a trauma response. Not feeling confident enough to trust my feelings, I need yours too.

Safety and validation were craved as a child. That child is still alive and well. I'm learning to care for and nurture her. She had a very hard time in life, and no one cared to keep her safe or listen to her. I keep her story alive.

Negative thinking is helpful to explore the world around us positively. Negative thinking does not mean the same as negativity. "Negativity" is a chronic attitude of anger, cynicism, despair, or hopelessness, in all or many situations. It's an overriding sense of doom and gloom. Nothing is ever right or good enough.

Negative thinking allows us the opportunity to view the potential dark side of people, places, ideas, and things in order to view them more honestly and realistically. To properly discern a situation.

Negative thinking can be an invaluable survival tool that helps us to thrive in life. Negative thinking can help us imagine the worst possible scenario and possible ways of avoiding it. It also helps us to set proper boundaries.

It's also important to take the proper time necessary to make well-thought-out choices. Considering the negative and positive aspects of a situation helps in this process.

This "negative" thinking helps us to look at ourselves and others more realistically. It helps to see injustices taking place and motivates one to make important improvements or necessary changes.

Negative thinking is actually "critical thinking." When you think critically you are less likely to fall for all claims or harmful assumptions, or even accept excuses. If we can't see what's wrong, we can't make it right. Negative thoughts are essential to our well-being and mental health. Suppressing negative thoughts and emotions means we cannot accurately evaluate our personal experiences in life. Suppressing such thoughts can also backfire and lower our sense of happiness and security.

Accepting negative thoughts can add clarity and understanding to our lives. If we do not accept the negatives in life it will become equally difficult to appreciate the positives in life. Society is biased towards thinking positively. It makes those who value negative thinking feel bad and embarrassed about negative emotions and thoughts. Shaming falls into the negativity category.

Being constantly positive is unrealistic and carries risks related to false motions and undoing stress from a lack of understanding and evaluating negativity.

It is important to accept negative thoughts and emotions. In learning to tolerate strong emotions and not rush to change our emotional state, we grow emotionally strong and confident. This strategy can help us cope in life as negative thoughts are essential to our survival. This raises one's emotional IQ.

God expects us to be sober-minded and aware at all times. Negative thinking is a tool given by God. We are called to use good judgment and discernment. This is perfectly taught to us through scripture. We are to have a critical eye towards life and use negative critical thinking as needed for honest assessment.

Don't be harassed into believing you're "negative" when in reality you are assessing life and your personal circumstances through a negative or critical lens. The Cross is negative, but we don't turn from it in favor of a more positive approach to Christ's death. It is ugly and painful and exactly where we are called to be witnesses.

That is not negativity. Be positively negative.

Perfectly Positive Pammie!

HORRORS AND ATROCITIES

I've experienced some gruesome things in life. I don't feel it's important to impart all the gory details though. One can imagine for themselves and might get pretty close to my reality.

Choices about how we react to traumas can make or break us. We can become bitter and sad, or we can choose to embrace our past, even if it was horrific. Not choose to love it but accept it and not continue to stare at it and obsess over it or resurrect it for special occasions.

This requires hard work and may take many years or even a lifetime to work through. Happiness, even in small increments, is still a measure of happiness worth having.

When someone is very young, it's easy to assume that there has to be something very wrong with you, for abuse to be taking place in your very small world. It's hard to formulate a different perspective that is bigger than you and not even really about you.

A child has no way to know or compare their parents against others. They can't tell that their parents are messing up their parenting job in ways that harm their children.

While healing from your childhood trauma, you may become aware you're cleaning up someone else's mess. A mess you didn't ask for, that now requires learning special skills to rid yourself of difficult and unwanted behaviors. Even though you may have genuine resentment about doing so, it's better to clean up a mess you didn't make, than to continue to exist in it.

Uncovering and knowing the truth can be painful but not knowing can be crippling. The reason for this is because you aren't living in the past, the past is living in you. It causes significant damage in all areas of life. A victim is operating out of a series of responses to trauma that includes self-preservation and countless protective measures. It's easy to chase away people you love with all the protective gear needed for survival.

Someone who is hyper-focused on survival will do what is necessary to stay safe physically and emotionally. These strategies are dysfunctional too and are not always considered helpful in the long run. Trauma and abuse responses seem to address an immediate need but often create lasting issues and conflicts.

Along with everything I suffered as a child, the abuse carried over into my teen years and adult life also. When I was sixteen, I almost died as a result of attempted murder.

On a Friday during school, I decided with a few other girlfriends to pan handle money from students in order to get a case of beer. In Ohio the drinking age was eighteen and I could always get a senior to buy a case for me.

Our plans were to go into the city and party at a friend's apartment who had graduated the previous year. We drove into the city with our beer and wine. It was the dead of winter with several feet of snow on the ground. This is significant to the story.

I'm one of those people who start drinking and don't stop until I black out. I'm fearless and will do all things risky, stupid and dangerous. At the gathering I began to drink like a fish. I lost all my inhibitions and any sense of danger.

Eventually I drank myself into an unconscious state but not before engaging in behavior I would not have, if I were sober. I was completely defenseless and at the mercy of those around me.

At some point, I woke up. I was lying on the floor on my back. I was being straddled by a boy sitting on me using both fists, punching in my face. I did not feel any pain, but my head was being bashed in and flopping back and forth with every blow.

Eventually I passed out again.

The next time I recall being conscious, I was in the kitchen being tortured. I mercifully passed out again.

What took place next was only glimpses and bits and pieces of the story from people who were present.

I continued to be beat and tortured. I will clarify that it was primarily one individual who was hurting me. In truth, he was trying to murder me.

At some point I was stripped naked and dumped into a cold tub of water. Later I was dragged outside naked and wet deep into the woods and left to die.

The only reason I'm still alive is one girl at the party got curious about what had happened to me and followed the trail in the snow from me being dragged into the woods. I was found.

This is nothing short of a God intervention. I'm not sure of anything else that took place as I did not regain consciousness until the next day.

I woke up in my friend's bed.

At age 17 while a senior, I met a college boy and began a long- distance relationship that lasted the majority of the year. His college was an hour away from me. I frequently ditched school and hitchhiked to his campus.

I was in the most dangerous relationship I'd ever been in. I was being tortured. The only physical encounters were forced. They occurred only in compromising places where there was a risk of being seen or caught. That was a titillating respect for him. The physical torture was excruciating but created a far deeper dilemma for me. It messed with my emotions and triggered all my childhood abuse.

Nothing was redeeming about him. He wasn't particularly handsome, kind, or flattering. Sometimes I felt he was jealous of me, but I was not certain why. His cruelty also led him to regularly cheat on me. His cheating hurt me more physically than his torture did. I often felt I wouldn't survive the emotional pain.

I've been asked repeatedly why I stayed in the relationship. I had one answer. Tonic immobility. It is a typical response to trauma. One either is frozen in place or has a fight-or-flight response. I was always physically and emotionally paralyzed by abuse. I also get very quiet and often become catatonic.

The most disturbing outcome in therapy was a therapist who repeatedly admonished me for staying in the relationship and desired the sexual details of the torture. I do not ever speak of those details to anyone. The fact that the issue repeatedly surfaced began to disturb me. I left him because I was no longer safe in his presence.

I'd become the victim of a sexual voyeur.

DANGER, DANGER

Accidents happen, so they say. I do question the nature of an accident though. Was there truly an accident or something born from negligence? If it's the result of negligence, it doesn't quite fit the unpredictability of an accident.

Our first family accident that I can remember was when I was 3 ½. My mother and sister and I lived alone in a two-room apartment. My sister and I slept in a bed together and my mother slept on the couch.

I woke up one morning with the house full of smoke. I went looking for my mother. I found her asleep on the couch. The reality of it was she passed out from drinking. She had no pillow or blankets and was in her regular clothes. Her head was resting on the arm of the couch. The entire arm of the couch had burned away and was continuing a slow process of smoldering itself out of existence.

I could not wake my mom for several minutes and the red smoldering flame was growing. Finally, she came slowly out of her stupor and realized the problem. She did not call the fire department but continued to pour water on the couch until the smoke finally stopped. She had fallen asleep with a lit cigarette. There was no ashtray to be found. My mother aired out the house and wrapped up the arm of the couch and we didn't skip a beat.

That was the first miracle I ever witnessed. My mother's head was lying on a smoldering disintegrating couch and she was untouched by it. We weren't all dead.

My next encounter with death was also at age three. Our neighbor had older daughters and an above ground swimming pool. The liner was black not blue. One hot summer day I was taken swimming in the pool. I didn't swim and couldn't touch the bottom. There were at least 8-10 children in the pool. I was left to cling to the sides.

At some point I went underwater. No one even noticed. I sank all the way to the bottom of the pool in all its darkness. I was not at all afraid but instinctively knew I was going to die. I had not been missed nor could I be seen. I closed my eyes and began drowning. I had gotten my body turned around, so I was facing the sky. I couldn't see it, but bright streaming sunlight was hitting the water and me.

A few minutes later I was hoisted out of the water and flopped onto the ground. I gasped for air. Again, I had survived death, only to be yelled at for letting go of the side of the pool.

Was anyone in charge of my life? It seemed no earthly presence was.

I became a very calm little person in the face of danger. Someone had to be. My mother was useless in a crisis. She was more intent on acting as if the crisis never occurred. She was the cover up and deny anything that happened in person.

So, I now have a second job in life. My first job title was that of babysitter. My next job assignment was head of crisis management.

My resume was growing. I'm pretty sure I shouldn't have had any jobs at all until I started school. Then my job was to finish my daily homework assignments. Kids should not be born with jobs. Even the job of loving a parent.

More "accidents" were to come. I rose to every occasion as the calm in the storm.

My baby brother, only 1 year old, choked on a piece of paper. I was the only one home with him. He began to turn a frightening blue color. I tried everything to clear his airway. Finally, I jammed my hand down his throat and retrieved the paper. He started breathing again. Michael was alive because I listened, and God provided a way.

Next incident was while my mother was doing laundry in the garage. I was home for lunch from school. My mother was holding my baby brother and put him down on the garage floor to free her hands. She set down an open bottle of bleach next to my brother who picked it up and drank it.

He immediately began to choke. My mother scooped him up and ran into the kitchen with him. I picked up the bleach bottle to read the instructions if ingested. I then went to the kitchen where my mom had poured milk and was trying to get my brother to drink it. I told her to stop. The bottle said not to induce vomiting or give milk. She was about to make things worse or even kill him. We lived three doors down from the fire station and I took my brother there. He was in the hospital a few days but lived. I had saved his life twice.

Many more accidents occurred. Children hit by cars, missing children that required search parties. Broken bones and teeth. Almost burned to death in several fires. Too many car accidents to mention.

My brother Philip died in a car accident. He was married with two daughters. We discovered upon his death the reality of my stepfather's abuse on him. We found his kiddie porn on his computer and boxes of it in his house. He did not have a current driver's license because he didn't have a birth certificate. He worked under a fake name. He had also been arrested as a peeping Tom on several occasions. He was a menace. I'm glad God saw fit to take him but so sorry for his impossible life.

Damage from abuse becomes generational. Victims create more victims. A disgusting and disheartening outcome for everyone. I have no doubt my nieces were affected by abuse due to their current behavior.

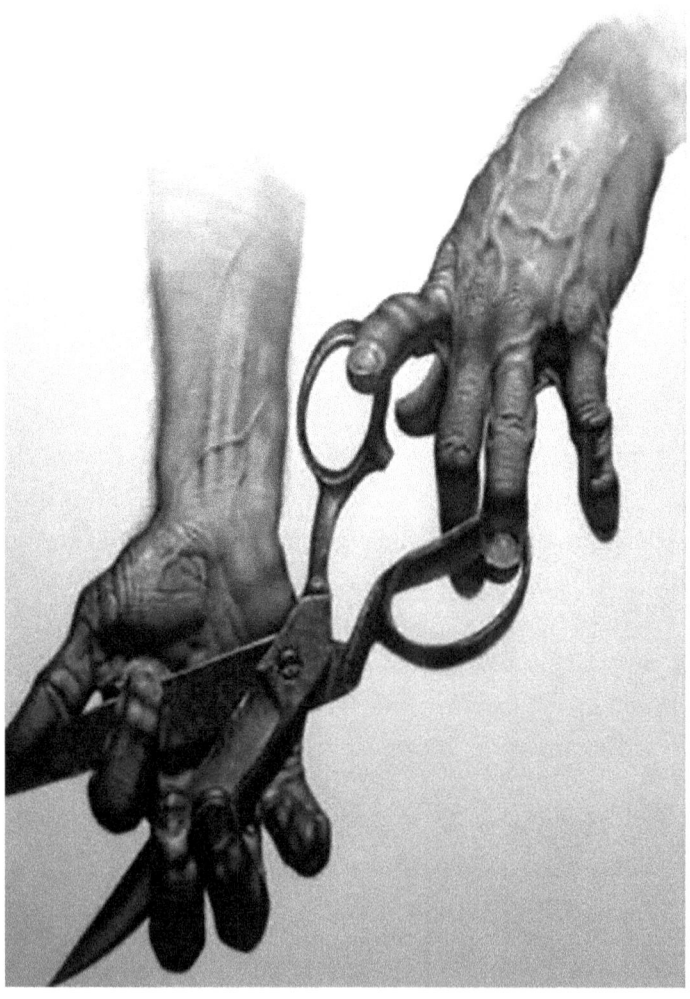

BELIEVING THE LIES

We will believe in lies when we feel too threatened or vulnerable to allow the truth and its aftermath to occupy space in our lives. When truth does surface, we often feel betrayed and we question our own ability to see things accurately.

A pathological liar will become extremely angry when proof of their falsehoods is found. They will become annoyed with minor questions about their fabrications. Most pathological liars start to believe their own lies even when confronted with proof of their falsehoods. They often balk at innocent questions about their fabrications. Many pathological liars believe their lies and find it effortless to lie rather than tell the truth. If you confront or question them, they become angry and hostile.

There are many case studies that indicate people will tend to seek out information that will confirm their beliefs do not disprove them. If the truth is revealed then it may require someone to take undesired action. They would have to change their narrative.

There are so many secrets and lies in my family, it's difficult to quantify them. I've sought the truth my entire existence. There are many truths uncovered or known that I do not share. One person alone. My sister Claire is the only sibling that I speak openly too about everything I know or surmise.

Claire has spent years securing the paper trail that tells the correct and legal version of the stories and lies. Together, we are a force that doesn't stop at "no."

Where Claire and I start to fall apart is with boundaries. I tend to swing back and forth between being a doormat and letting people walk all over me, or being a fortress, locking people out.

Both behaviors are driven by fear. Fear of losing people and fear of getting too close. Healing is the middle ground where you can let people be close but also hold them to expectations by setting boundaries. That is where you find authentic love from people who love and respect you.

SO YOU DON'T LIKE ME?

I have lots of enemies and frenemies. I also have people who love me. I'm aware of both. Those who dislike me generally fall into two different categories but for the same reasons on both sides.

The first big reason is I'm always working on my stuff. Second, I'm smart. Both are intimidating for obvious reasons and a deadly combination with relatives. Being smart in itself isn't a reason to be disliked but letting people know I'm smart because of my insecurity about being dumb bugs' people.

Some behaviors would lead you to think I'm pretty stupid. Not so. I'm often slow to react to abuse but eventually I catch on. A lot of what I do in those situations are trauma responses. To people who don't understand or are victims themselves, this is a difficult conversation that they just don't get. I can explain till I'm blue in the face.

I've come very far in recovery. I've never remarried, which has probably saved my life. I work hard at being well but have stopped explaining myself to people who don't care. That's similar to trying to convince people I'm a different person. One has to actually live their lives differently, not explain it differently.

Some people are frazzled by complicated stories that include trauma and abuse, addictions and mental health issues. They don't make good listeners and are known to run from you and avoid you. Don't take this personally. It's not about you, it's about them. How other people behave is always about them.

God will place people in your life, those up who are interested in you and love you. You will be amazed at the different ways God will use you and your story to Glorify Him.

Our stories are powerful in that we have been rescued by God. I have a deeper need and relationship with God than I've ever had. I'm so honored to be constantly fed by His Word. Joyful I'm able to write devotionals and write about life in relationship to God. Through my writing, I'm continually being spoken to and schooled on God and His ways by reading what He has instructed us to read. The Bible.

Not so long ago, I would have been very upset if someone didn't like me or ended our friendship. I'd search deep within myself for what I'd done to cause it. It had to be me who caused it.

In making a decision to be well, I had to eliminate the self-talk that was connected to negativity. To stop obsessing over losses and accept any part I may have played and not pressure people to like me. Certainly, there are people I don't care for. I'm entitled to have my feelings and so is everyone else.

Chicago 1970.

SUICIDE DETERMINATION

There have been two successful suicides in my family. Death by gunshot. Suicide is more successful with men. They do not as a rule discuss their plans. I've known one exception to that rule. My friend Larry, who for months engaged everyone he could in a discussion on the pros and cons of suicide. His issue was his family's expectations of him. He was expected to attend medical school and it wasn't what he wanted. He won the argument by suicide, but we lost an important wonderfully kind human as a result. I cried for days. I didn't understand how we had all had the suicide conversation with him and it never clicked that he was taking a poll. He was looking for an answer to his suicidal thoughts. He wanted a way to live his life according to his desires and not lose his family's support as a result.

On January 7th, 2019, I made one of the biggest decisions of my life. It was not made lightly or on a whim. I had finally, for the last time, reached my expiration date. I was done. I wanted to leave this world, permanently.

I have had suicidal feelings in the past. I also had stockpiled medications just in case, but never before tried to die. Reaching a place where I was unable to cope any longer, my head hurt from life. I wanted out and saw this as a blessing to everyone in my life. I have heard many people refer to those who successfully ended their lives, that it's the coward's way out, meaning too, the easy way. Let me explain. There is nothing easy about making that decision. To end one's life requires bravery you may never understand.

No one ever wants to be dead. They just want out of their emotional pain. If you look at suicide this way then it's easy to see that the act of suicide is accidental. People are in pain, reaching for the wrong solution to a seemingly impossible situation. The definition of an accident is "an unfortunate incident." That sums up suicide nicely.

When I was determined to die, I began to carefully plan my method. I was either going to overdose or jump off our local bridge, that was not survivable. This was a common way for people to suicide.

The thought of dying in my bed was more comforting. I had sleeping pills on hand but not enough. I had a small amount of pain medicine handy for an upcoming surgery. I just needed more.

Working on the problem, I got a refill prescription for more sleep medications. I also went to my psychiatrist and begged for psych meds stating I was not well. I do not routinely use psych meds due to the side effects and neurological damage I've already encountered. I pleaded desperation.

When I finally had a significant quantity of deadly pills on hand, I was satisfied. I had 220 sleep, pain, and anti-psychotic medications that would do the job I needed them for. The date I chose to end my life was January 9th.

On January 8, I saw my psychologist. I did not want to be stopped from my approaching plan. Somehow, I ended up telling my therapist exactly what I was up to. I explained I googled the best time to jump off the bridge and had an all- essential stash of drugs. He laughed at me. He laughed at me. He said it was now impossible to jump off the bridge because they raised the security fencing by 6 feet.

The truth is, since raising that fence, it has created a bit of an inconvenience but has not been a deterrent. People simply bring a ladder with them now.

I saw this blatant dismissal as the supporting green light I needed to proceed as planned. I went home even sadder and more resigned to dying.

Do not think or assume that ending one's life is cowardly. I can't begin to describe the courage it takes to die. I also do not view suicide as a sin. The desire to die is a symptom of deep psychological pain and illness. I view suicide as always accidental. I don't believe suicides are genuinely seeking death. That are genuinely seeking an end to their pain. Emotional instability and emotional pain are far greater than physical pain. I live with both and will take the physical pain any day over the emotional kind.

It's a scary decision to make, ending one's, life and I had a few days to sit on. As the minutes and hours passed, I became more and more reconciled to the process. There was excitement and resolve to make up my mind. I almost felt happy about the decision.

I made one last attempt at reaching out. I called my oldest daughter to make a request. The request was not unreasonable, and it was something I needed that may have halted my death plan.

My daughter was utterly incensed at my request. I was chastised and humiliated that I dared to request at all. She was misinformed about what she thought my request entailed and refused to listen to any reasonable account I could extoll.

She was mean, hateful, patronizing, and very wrong. She said everything I needed to hear to support my decision to die. I did not want these hassles in my life any longer. I had made the right decision and now was solidly aligned with my plan.

Let me be very clear here. I did not try to kill myself because my daughter was unkind to me. I'd pretty much resolved to kill myself already. What I was looking for was a reason not to kill myself and I could not find one. Life had simply become too hard for me. I was tired and wanted out.

I wrote notes to loved ones I kept on my cell phone. I was ready to die. I got out all my pills. I even took anti-nausea medication to avoid vomiting up the drugs. I did not want any hiccups.

While swallowing my pills one at a time, my oldest daughter called me again. She wanted to know if I was OK. She said she sensed I was angry. Seriously! I assured her I was fine. I did not wish to linger on the phone. I was on a mission. The mission was my death.

I do not know how many sleeping pills I took, but I left the psych meds behind, feeling confident the sleep meds and narcotics would do the job. I was ready to be gone. I fell into a deep sleep.

In the morning, I woke up. I was astonished. How was it that I was still alive? It couldn't be possible. I got up and dressed and made a smoothie. When I was finished, I swallowed 120 psych meds.

The following events are sketchy but to the best of my ability to recall.

I remember being in my bathroom on the floor in the dark, yelling for my aunt. I was in terrible pain. What I thought was taking place was that I was being held hostage by an intruder.

Eventually, I changed locations. In my living room, I could hear people talking in the garden outside my balcony. I could not stand or walk but was crawling on the carpet. I was aware something was very wrong but did not remember taking all the pills. I just remembered being held hostage.

Crawling on the floor was in actuality me trying to propel myself forward by pulling myself through the carpet with my arms. The result of that was I literally scraped off all the skin on my arms in the process.

I lay in the hall where I had a view into my bedroom and watched the police make their way in. My bed with sizable headboard washes up against my window. My nightstand was next to it.

Eventually the police got in by trampling over my bed. The first thing they noticed were the empty pill bottles. I explained I had just run out. They were smart enough to notice the prescriptions were just recently filled. I finally agreed I took all the pills but was fine because I wasn't dead.

Upon hearing the voices outside, I began to yell for help. I was asking whoever was there to call 911. Eventually the police did come. They tried to communicate with me through my open bedroom window. My front door was locked, and they were trying to get me to unlock it. I was still unable to stand or walk. Crawling over to the front door, I attempted to reach the door lock, but was unsuccessful.

I am certain any instructions given to me by the police were probably impossible for me to implement. I sat next to the front door and waited for the police to try and get into my apartment through the cracked window.

They finally got through and had the ambulance EMT's access the situation and get me to the hospital. There they did cat scans and pushed my bed into a cubicle where I stayed for three days. None of my wounds were addressed and I was virtually ignored.

I was missing so much skin that I stuck to the sheets like glue. To turn I had to endure the pain of separating myself from the bed linens. I had not seen myself in a mirror. My eyes were black and blue, much of the skin on my face was missing and my neck was black and blue from ear to ear. I was told by a nurse I had tried to hang myself.

90% of my body was black and blue with open wounds as deep and wide as 8 inches by 2 inches. Previous scars on my body from different surgeries had ruptured open. I had knots on my head the size of goose eggs. What in the world had taken place?

For three long days, I stayed in the ER. I later found out I had a DNR on file. The hospital did not think I would survive. I quietly cried when no one was watching.

To add to my growing list of medical problems was my inability to feed myself, bathe myself, or dress myself. Eventually, I developed a pronounced stutter. My intestines quit working. No one seemed to care at the hospital.

A social worker showed up once a day for a few minutes, but I don't even remember much about that until the final day when she said I was going to be transported several hours away to a hospital. I became hysterical. I wanted to go back home.

When the ambulance arrived to take me, they wanted to change my dirty gown. It was then that the complete extent of my wounds was noticed. They were not going to transport me without being properly bandaged. Someone finally cared.

Three hours later I arrived at my new destination. It was a real hospital that had a psychiatric floor. The first thing they did was take off all my clothes and photograph my entire body. Then they cleaned me up and began the ritual of twice-daily wound care.

Every nurse and aide assigned to me asked the same questions. How was all the damage done? I did not have any answers. I wish I knew what took place myself. I wish someone had a camera on me those two days. It must have been hell.

The following morning, I met with the psychiatrist in charge of my care. He had a file on me that stood nearly two feet high. I was amazed they had gotten so much information so quickly. One of the first things the doctor wanted to know from me was why I never reported sexual abuse to my mother. This doctor was going to be a hoot.

I explained that my mother was a drunk who did not have any interest in knowing anything about me. Then I laughed so hard I almost wet my pants. The doctor chastised me for taking 30 pills. I almost lost it. I'd taken 220 pills, and I wanted full credit for my effort.

Thirty pills would not have done anything. I was serious. I wanted to be dead. Not only was I alive but now I was dealing with problems caused by the overdose. That seemed like cruel and unusual punishment from God. I still desired to be dead. Now I was angry at God too. And so ensued the longest argument ever with my creator. It lasted for four months. He ultimately won.

Can God ever lose?

Even in my anger at God, I attempted obedience. When I finally got released from the hospital several weeks later, I committed myself to regularly attending church. I didn't want to be there but went anyway.

I would not sing the hymns or follow the service and liturgy but that didn't matter to God. He was speaking directly to my heart and soul through His Word. I was being fed through the service by being present. It didn't matter to God that I was upset about it. He had me right where He wanted me.

My children were furious at the suicide attempt. Personally, I refer to it as my suicide determination. It was not an attempt. I was serious about wanting to be dead. The only reason I'm not dead, is because that was not God's plan for me.

Each of us is completely dependent on God for every moment that we are alive. We are only alive because God keeps us breathing. God is in charge of preserving all life. He is doing what is in our best interest at all times.

God and I embarked on a new journey, with a new understanding. Life is undoubtedly the greatest gift God can give us. The greatest until you realize that eternal life is His perfection for us that is never-ending. God was going to make sure I never forgot who was in control. It is and was and always will be HIM.

Mental illness is not rude, wrong, or self-centered. If that were the case, then all physical ailments would be selfish too. Don't judge mental illness as a personality flaw. If you do, you need to rediscover the definition of illness. Mental illness deserves the same concern and respect as cancer or pneumonia.

Taken a few short months after my suicide determination.

THE DEATH WE DON'T DISCUSS

I was a very promiscuous teenager. This is the typical behavior of a sex abuse victim. Being a victim altered my understanding of love and sex and I easily confused sex as love. I never used birth control and never considered the possibility I could become pregnant. I began to think I couldn't get pregnant because I hadn't gotten pregnant. To be honest, it never really entered my mind what I'd do if a pregnancy became an issue.

That attitude is "so me." I was never thinking ahead. I just went through life merely acting and reacting. If a problem appeared, I dealt with it then and not before. I never anticipated trouble, I knew it was coming consistently and eventually. You don't grow up abused and traumatized without confidence that things are going to go badly. I felt jinxed in everything.

It was almost a year after I met my husband that I became pregnant. I wanted a baby and was excited by the prospect. However, no one in my world was going to support that plan. My future husband got pregnant with one of our housemates soon after he moved into our house. She too wanted to keep the baby but was successfully coerced into having an abortion. After that she left college and went back home where she spent time in a psychiatric hospital, despondent.

At the time of my pregnancy, we were facing some big decisions as a couple. His professor was moving to Texas and wanted Jose to follow him for the sake of educational continuity. I was not so sure it was a move I wanted to make. Now a pregnancy clouded and complicated the picture.

I desperately wanted to keep the baby. He adamantly disagreed. I went to a campus doctor who coincidently was also from Puerto Rico. He did not appreciate me at all. He saw me as a slut trying to hitch her wagon to a gravy train.

Since I was undecided about the move and wanted to keep my baby, I was taking lots of heat. Jose's professor hinted he needed a new more agreeable girlfriend. The pressure to abort was intense. I tried to get support from friends who felt it would be better to abort. As a last resort, I called my mother. I knew she would say the right thing. She didn't. She said I'd be better off having an abortion.

I was sad, alone, and expecting a human to be born from my body. I couldn't believe I was in the mess I was all alone. Jose came to me with an offer he felt I wouldn't refuse. He was working hard at emotional coercion. A nice word for emotional abuse. He said he would marry me if I got an abortion. I finally agreed. I accepted a marriage proposal in exchange for the murder of my child.

That single decision made the most profound impact on me, more than any other decision in my life. It became my heart's cry, my ministry, my purpose, and my direction. The fight I had fought so hard for, legalized abortion in every state, has been the catalyst for forgiveness and mercy for the last 41 years of my life.

I have also been blessed by seeing the seeds God used me to plant over the years grow mightily. Abortion kills innocent children and hurts women. That is where my passion lies. Teaching God's forgiveness where none is deserved.

After the abortion, I began to hemorrhage. I called the hospital for several days worried. They said it was normal and acted like I was bothering them. Almost a week later I began to hemorrhage so severely I thought I would bleed to death. I was weak and pale. I decided to call was no longer a working option. We did not have a car, but the emergency room was only about a mile away. I got dressed and walked there. They immediately concluded I was hemorrhaging to death. They asked why I hadn't gone in sooner. I was hysterical. I had to have another D&C. It was now only four days before my wedding day. I understood the ramifications of the procedure. No sex. I was getting married and could not have sex on that day.

It set the tone for every subsequent anniversary. Exactly nothing happened. It was barely acknowledged. To this day, nearly 50 years later, I can't remember the actual date anyway. That is how important our vows were to each other. We were going through the motions of a marriage not truly committed to the sacred union of holy matrimony. We did not even have wedding rings. What would be the point of that?

An unfortunate fact about abortion is your chances of staying with the person you aborted with are almost nonexistent. Murder has that effect on relationships. He had now aborted two children that I'm aware of.

Five months after my abortion I became pregnant again. I was so excited. I would not be talked out of this baby. I bought maternity clothes, and my mother even bought some baby clothes. I was finally going to get to hold my baby.

At four months pregnant I began to miscarry. I did not want to lose the baby. I rested and anxiously waited. I finally miscarried the baby at nearly four months. I had to have another D&C. I had now lost two children. More likely than not, the miscarriage of my second child was due to my uterus becoming a war zone from the abortion. Any good pro-abortion doctor or nurse will tell you that's hogwash. Every pro-life doctor or nurse will stand in agreement with that.

Though it was a huge disappointment and loss, I did not have the same reaction as I did with the abortion. Several months after the abortion I suffered from post-abortion psychosis.

I continued to work and go to school. I knew that children would somehow be in my future. I was very anxious to have them. Several years after my abortion, I became pregnant for the third time during a visit from friends in Wisconsin who had two daughters. I was glad to have the visit until they actually arrived. When they did arrive, each of the children was sick. Colds, flu, who knew? I just knew they weren't well.

I was worried about this pregnancy and did not want to lose another child. Before I even knew I was expecting a baby, I had become quiet myself. I could barely breathe or get out of bed. Fortunately, it was during spring break from school, so I wasn't missing much.

I was seeing our doctor about every other day for injections. I had come down with pneumonia. I was prescribed additional medicine along with antihistamines. It took nearly a month to regain my strength and that is when I realized I was pregnant.

I was so concerned for the baby with all the medications I'd taken. Some were very dangerous for the baby in the early stages of development. Things went relatively smoothly until the fourth month. I began to have trouble which in turn created anxiety.

I became an unwelcome pest to my doctor. At one point I called him worried sick over undesirable symptoms and my doctor, in his frustration and unprofessional way, asked me if I'd just rather have an abortion. I was appalled by the suggestion and vowed to not return to that doctor again.

Ten years after my abortion I went to an abortion healing group. There my lost child's dignity was restored. She was no longer a blob of tissue discarded in the garbage and I have come to know the healing hand of God's forgiveness. So much so, that I made it my life's mission to support post-abortive women. I created a post-abortion recovery group that I have now facilitated for twenty years.

God can and does forgive everything. Jesus did not die on the cross for everyone except women who aborted their children. Sin is sin. As much as we are tempted to rank sins from best to worst, God does not view sin that way.

Though Christ loves and forgives us He does not prevent us from experiencing the consequences of our sin. He simply holds us tight so that we might feel His presence and know of His undeserved mercy and Grace.

God longs to wash us white as snow. He alone is capable of accomplishing that. We do not even possess the ability to forgive ourselves as self-forgiveness is not ours to grant. If self- forgiveness was all that was required, Christ did not need to go to the cross on our behalf. But He did. It Is finished.

Many years ago, I wrote a letter to my children in heaven. This is it.

To my babies:

I want you to know how much you are loved. How much I wanted you and yet, you are not here with me today. The reason for that is because of my selfishness.

Our Father fearfully and wonderfully created you in Heaven. You are children who our Lord knows intimately and lovingly breathed life into. Our Father in Heaven formed you and gave you to me with much thought and deliberation. We are a perfect match. Though you are created in His image to have His smile and His spirit in your heart, you are also part of me. If you were to look into a mirror, you would see God and I looking back at you. But you are not here.

You may be wondering why I am not holding you in my arms and stroking your hair. Why I do not tuck you into bed at night and say your prayers to you. The reason why I cannot kiss your sweet faces is because I took your lives from you.

I was unable to trust the Lord enough in my own life, to have welcomed you into it. I was afraid and insecure about who I was and who God was. I lacked the wisdom and the strength to protect you and defend your right to life and God's plan for each of you.

The pain and agony of that single decision have forever altered me. I have ached to hold you in my arms. To feel your heart beating against mine and to breathe in the sweet perfume of your baby's innocence.

Though I have grieved your loss, I now have the assurance that you are happy in someone else's arms. That Jesus plays with you every day and kisses your faces and strokes your hair and tucks you into bed at night.

I seek your forgiveness and God's forgiveness for the agonizing separation from you, which also separated me from God. But now, I too can rest in His arms and see glimpses of you through His eyes. I am now comforted that He cares for you more than I ever could have.

Jesus has freed me from everlasting sorrow and condemnation. God has given us everlasting hope, love, and life instead.

So, though we are not physically together, there will be a time when we will be reunited together in Heaven and we can each sit with Jesus, loving each other and stroking His hair and kissing His sweet face.

All thanks and glory and praise be to God. For His mercy and blessing know no bounds.

Loving you always, Mommy

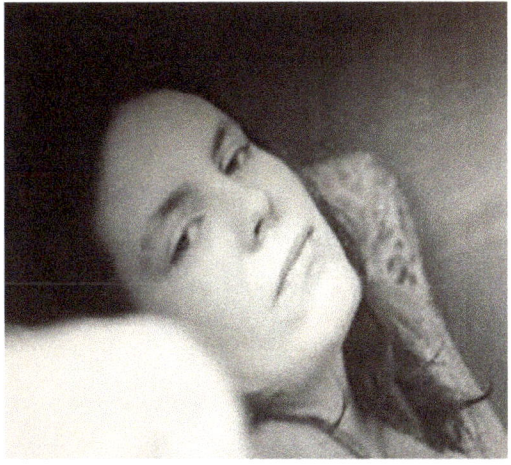

The saddest day in my life. My abortion.

Christ weeping with aborted baby. Auburn

117

I remember and give my lost children the respect and dignity they deserved on earth. I have named my children as I would my living children.

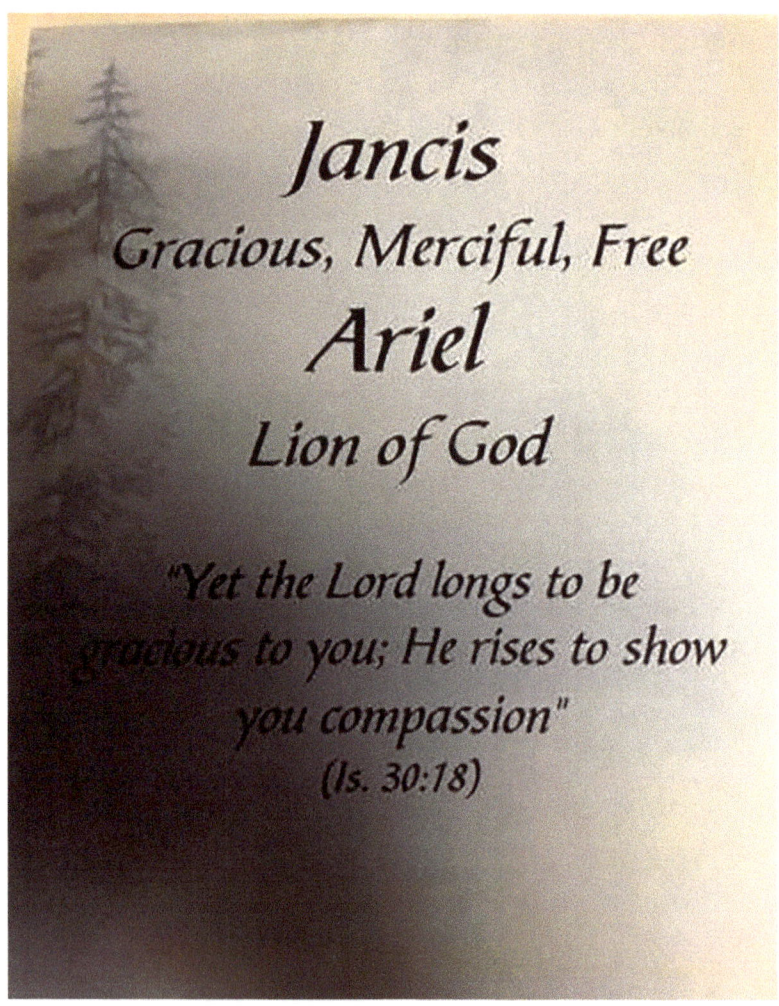

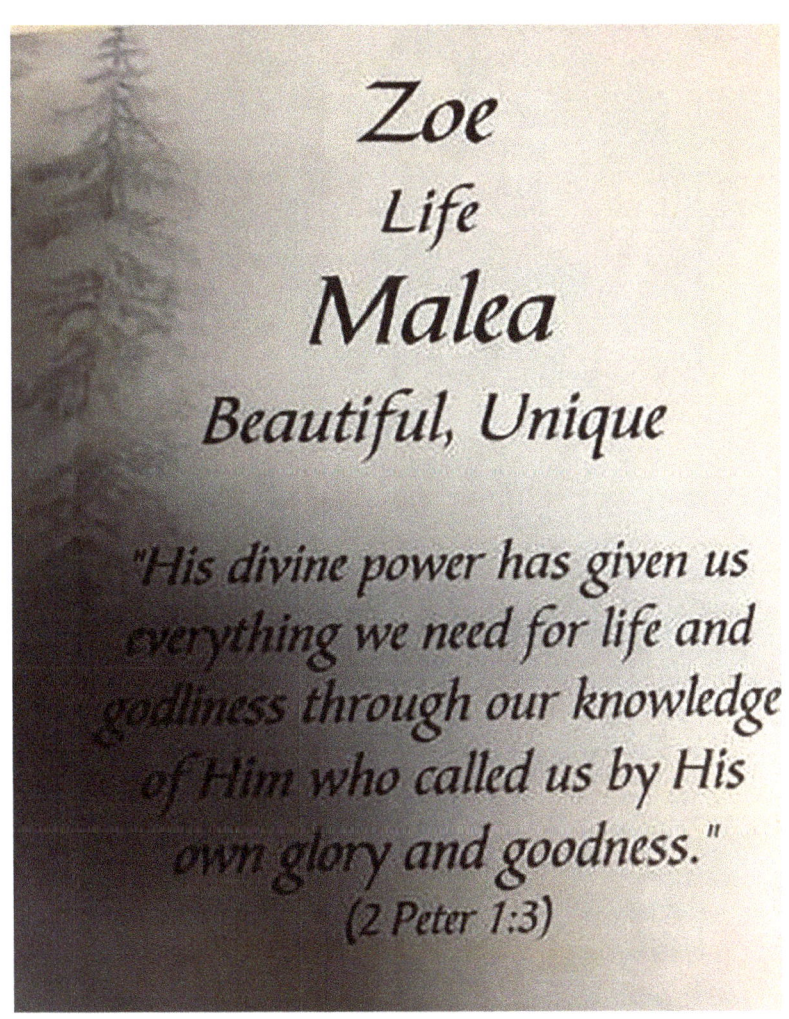

Zoe
Life
Malea
Beautiful, Unique

"His divine power has given us everything we need for life and godliness through our knowledge of Him who called us by His own glory and goodness."
(2 Peter 1:3)

FAR FAR AWAY

My first born was only a few months old as we packed for our move off the continent to live back on my husband's island. I was very apprehensive about moving so far away but as usual excited about the prospect of another new beginning.

All our furniture and belongings, including our car, had to be professionally crated for overseas shipping. It would take months for our things to reach us in Puerto Rico. We had shipped almost double the amount of furniture because we purchased new furniture to move with us and had everything shipped together.

We rented a house in Mayaguez. Our new next-door neighbors had a baby boy about the same age as our daughter. They were living in a house with barely any furnishings at all.

Upon the arrival of our household goods, we moved all our original furniture into the neighbor's house. I was glad it was going to good use. I was pleased that God put it on our hearts to take it with us.

It was difficult to adjust to the weather. It's extremely humid and there is no air conditioning built into the homes. It takes approximately one year to climatize to the humidity and eventually, you do. There are only two types of homes built in Puerto Rico. Either cinder block construction or wood homes. Wood homes are simply constructed by the poor inhabitants of the island. Nearly 70% of the population is poor and qualifies for food assistance. There are no additional subsidies from the government. Only food stamps.

There certainly was some culture shock. The male and female roles were different. Men did not listen to women. Women were in strict traditional roles. Unmarried girls on a date were chaperoned. I was a hippie and they did not exist in Puerto Rico. I was completely out of my element. There was no English programming on television. No American music to listen to.

We were staying with friends who we knew in the States. They had come to visit us in Texas from Wisconsin. While they were in our home our first daughter was conceived. Now in their home, our second daughter was conceived. You might say they were our good luck charms.

I had wanted another child right away. I wanted diapers and baby toys all at the same time. I didn't want to stretch it out forever, and so I became pregnant again. I was elated to have another child but not anxious for another difficult pregnancy.

I found an OBGYN, and he started me on monthly shots of a medication I know absolutely nothing about. It was supposed to help me not to miscarry. It did its job splendidly.

When it came time to pick a date for delivery the doctor wished to schedule the C-Section towards the middle of February out maybe another week. I explained to the doctor I couldn't have a baby born in February. The doctor explained that the baby would come in February whether I liked it or not.

I firmly stood my ground and scheduled the delivery for March 1. The doctor assured me the baby would come sooner than that. I shook my head no. On March 1st my second daughter was scheduled to be delivered and she did not disappoint me.

Many years later after receiving post-abortion counseling, I wondered why I was so adamant about my baby's due date being in March. I counted out when my aborted child would be born. That baby would have arrived in February. I was holding the month sacred in that baby's honor.

Home from the hospital with my second daughter, she was introduced to her big sister who promptly changed her name, and it has stuck to this day. She does not even respond to the name on her birth certificate.

My happy place, Buye! Puerto Rico

WRATH

Are you angry! Good! Anger is an honest emotion. Anger is not a sin if you handle it properly. God speaks to us about being angry in His Word.

He helps us to understand this important emotion and how to properly acknowledge and resolve it.

The reality of anger is that it truly is hurt, emotional pain. Anger can easily morph into wrath without proper consideration and a conversation with God.

Ephesians 4:26
In your anger do not sin. Do not let the sun go down while you are still angry.

Anger is my easiest "go too" emotion. When 80% of your life has been atrocious, anger is a perfectly understandable fit. I'm comfortable being angry as it is what I'm most familiar with. Anger and I are on intimate terms. We speak the same language. I've had plenty to be angry at. It's not OK to pass judgment on what you don't know or haven't experienced. Don't allow others to tell you anger is wrong.

Sin causes brokenness not to anger. Anger can become a sin if we use it to be hurtful to others or ourselves. It's perfectly acceptable to tell someone you are angry with them. Attacking others because of anger is sinning.

It's easy to hold onto anger towards our abusers. It's also important to understand who is actually hurt by holding onto that anger (wrath). God's Word speaks to us about this subject so that we can be clear about our participation or part in all circumstances.

God's doctrine of wrath often experiences hard times in today's world. Any concept of "wrath" upsets our modern ideologies and is too disconcerting and intolerant to imagine. People don't want to deal with God's wrath, preferring a gentler and kinder God. This is an important mistake many make. This is the fundamental basis of many modern churches. More love, less sin acknowledged. Both are essential to understanding doctrine and God's Word.

Different groups even alter the Holy Scriptures to fit their beliefs. Many people have not read God's unadulterated Word.

Deuteronomy 12:32
"What thing soever I command you, observe to do it: thou shalt not add thereto, nor diminish from it."

In our current climate, it is common to judge God's character and put Him on trial. We question how can hell possibly be fair. Why would God tell the Israelites to destroy the Canaanites? Why does God get angry? God is supposed to always be loving and kind. So many people struggle with this that now more than ever, we need to understand the proper meaning regarding these issues and God's doctrine of wrath.

God's wrath is just, prudent, and necessary. It is in accord with His perfect justice. God's wrath is in proportion to man's sinfulness. We can assume God's wrath is deserved when we are on the receiving end of it.

Romans 2:5
But because of your hard impenitent heart, you are storing up wrath for yourself on the day of wrath when God's righteous judgment will be revealed.

God's wrath is also His love in action in our lives. The action is against sin. God's wrath is never the capricious, self-indulgent, irritable, or immoral repugnant thing that human wrath often involves. It is a righteous and necessary reaction to our evil and sinfulness.

Proverbs 24:12
If you say, behold we did not know this, does not He who weighs the heart perceive it? Does not He who keeps watch over your soul know it, and not repay man according to his work?

God's wrath is meant to be feared. Because we all have sinned and fallen short of God's glory, His wrath is to be feared as we are justly condemned sinners apart from Christ. In actuality, we do not always get the wrath we deserve. It is because God is not fair. If He were, we would get what we deserve. Total inhalation.

Romans 1:18
For the wrath of God is revealed from Heaven against all ungodliness and unrighteousness of men, who by their unrighteousness suppress the truth.

God must act justly and judge sin or He would not be God. God's wrath is His love against sin. God is love and He does all things for His glory. God rules, restores, and judges in a way that brings Him maximum glory.

Revelations 19:15
From his mouth comes a sharp sword with which to strike down the nations, and he will rule them, with a rod of iron. He will tread the wine press of the fury of the wrath of God the Almighty.

God's wrath is satisfied in Christ. We have the ultimate good news, that God saved us from His wrath, He rescued us from what we could not do ourselves, and He accomplished what we as sinners didn't deserve.

Matthew 10:28
And do not fear those who kill the body but cannot kill the soul. Rather fear him who can destroy both soul and body in hell.

God's wrath is in response to ungodliness, wickedness, stubbornness, unrepentant hearts, and those who reject Jesus as Savior. God is right and just in doing so as He is the judge of all mankind. God is always in charge and deals with individuals according to their needs.

God gives us the freedom to make our own decisions about how we live. In that process, we also choose the consequences.

Romans 6:23
For the wages of sin is death, but the free gift of God is eternal life in Christ Jesus our Lord.

God can be love and exact wrath at the same time. In experiencing God's principles at work, we also come to know His grace, mercy, favor, and answer to prayer. Faithful lessons learned on our journey to knowing God.

Romans 9:22-23
What if God, desiring to show his wrath and make known his power, has endured with much patience the vessels of wrath made for destruction, to make known the riches of his glory for the vessels of mercy which he has prepared beforehand for his glory, even us whom he has called, not from the Jews only but also from the Gentiles.

God's wrath is precise and controlled in response to disobedience and disregard of His Holiness. His rage is not unfair, reckless or senseless vengeance on the innocent. Those who perish because of God's wrath are receiving what they deserve, not because God is a bully who happened to lose His temper. One rightfully earns the wrath of God.

Luke 16:19-31

"There was a rich man who was dressed in purple and fine linen and lived in luxury every day.(At his gate was laid a beggar(named Lazarus, covered with sores and longing to eat what fell from the rich man's table.(Even the dogs came and licked his sores.

"The time came when the beggar died, and the angels carried him to Abraham's side. The rich man also died and was buried. In Hades, where he was in torment, he looked up and saw Abraham far away, with Lazarus by his side. So he called to him, 'Father Abraham,(D) have pity on me and send Lazarus to dip the tip of his finger in water and cool my tongue because I am in agony in this fire.'

"But Abraham replied, 'Son, remember that in your lifetime you received your good things, while Lazarus received bad things,(F)but now he is comforted here and you are in agony.(And besides all this, between us and you a great chasm has been set in place, so that those who want to go from here to you cannot, nor can anyone cross over from there to us.'

"He answered, 'Then I beg you, father, send Lazarus to my family, for I have five brothers. Let him warn them,(H) so that they will not also come to this place of torment.'

"Abraham replied, 'They have Moses(I) and the Prophets;(J) let them listen to them.'

"'No, Father Abraham,'(K) he said, 'but if someone from the dead goes to them, they will repent.'

"He said to him, 'If they do not listen to Moses and the Prophets, they will not be convinced even if someone rises from the dead.'"

God's wrath.

WEAPONS OF CHOICE

My family, including extended family has perfected the art of war. They've honed their skills on the heels of generations. They even possess weapons of mass destruction. Their most destructive and most frequently used weapon is the "silent treatment." Depending on the duration of the punishment, it is hard to determine the full scope of the effects, but even short stints of this weapon are detrimental to anyone on the receiving end.

Other weapons of war are "destruction of property." Then there is" theft of property," always followed by, finders' keepers, losers, weepers. Rage is used frequently. We can't ignore the classic passive-aggressive. When rage does not work, an all-out tantrum might do the trick. Mental and emotional abuse are the weapons of last resort, used after or in tandem with "the silent treatment. Narcissists enlist "flying monkeys." Recruiting others into the fray to continue their war as good soldiers.

There are no rules of war. Anything goes. This applies to totally unsuspecting strangers. Strangers who may just be caught in the crossfire or become the actual target.

Not only is "war" effective, regarding its proliferation of victims, it can sometimes be amusing and entertaining. I spent one Thanksgiving, watching my son-in-law in a knockdown, drag-out fistfight with his brother-in-law on the front lawn. I have no idea what precipitated the event but it certainly fit the day. Working in the kitchen was Grandie, cussing out anyone who went in there. It was a typical holiday spent with dysfunctional nincompoops.

I have several siblings who have repeatedly been banned from businesses because of bad behavior. One sister even hit an employee. I have numerous scars received from acts of war that became acts of violence.

I do not do well, respond well, or cope well when any of these tactics or weapons are in play. I do not initiate war or participate in it. The mentality of war is dangerous and creates wounds that are not easily healed. Since I'm a Fawn, I'm forever cleaning up the messes and explaining away the bad behavior when out in public with family members and friends who cannot play nicely.

What starts the wars, is "your guess is as good as mine." Wars have been started over something as innocuous as the mix-up of a sandwich order at a deli or as criminal as the theft of expensive jewelry.

That my family wars at all is my mother's strategy of divide and conquer. She worked tirelessly to keep us siblings at each other's throats and isolated from each other. Her fear was any of us asking each other questions and comparing notes. A cohesive and loving family could get to the bottom of things and support one another through difficult times. That is not how things were done growing up "Zissis."

Separating oneself from all the players to stay out of the direct line of fire is not an act of war. It is actually an act of bravery, worthy of a medal.

Silent treatment has become the mainstay and most destructive of all weapons used. I had the silent treatment used on me as a toddler. The use of silent treatment is not just to punish is primarily a weapon of control.

The silent treatment damages and leaves lasting effects on its victims. It does not allow for healthy communication. It's considered a form of neglect and prevents any and all accountabilities. It leaves in its wake psychological stress and emotional trauma upon its recipients. It's an unhealthy dynamic that enables control and has a dehumanizing effect.

Silence is equal to violence. It's designed to be a punishment. People employing this technique are not just refusing to talk to you, their intention is to not acknowledge you even exist. It's a way to inflict pain without leaving any physical marks. It's a form of aggression that dominates and manipulates. It denotes superiority over another human being. It's also a way to invalidate someone and end the discussion until the other person changes their thoughts to match their abusers. There is usually no explanation given for the silent treatment.

The silent treatment can last days, weeks, months, years, or until you're discarded altogether. There is never a good reason or logic behind the decision so don't try to understand it. The abusers who use it cannot regulate their emotions and have no empathy at all.

When children are repeatedly subjected to silent treatment, they in turn learn helplessness, shame, and what it feels like to be invisible.

When on the receiving end of the silent treatment you will be, blocked, and not have calls answered or returned. All forms of communication will cease. This happens to give you the feeling that you're crazy and the abuser needs to protect themselves from you. It's an attempt to try and mentally break you.

Stepping away from unhealthy or toxic relationships is not using silent treatment. That is taking care of yourself. You can retreat from abusive and toxic relationships without explanation. People know what they did, you don't need to give the breakdown of their bad behavior. That only serves to try and justify your departure to someone who will ultimately blame you anyway. Walk away silently.

Having your personal property stolen or destroyed works the same way as the silent treatment. It's a statement of control and manipulation. I visited home once when my daughter was a baby. While there, I misplaced an expensive gold and turquoise earring that was a gift from my husband. I looked everywhere for it, though I was certain it had disappeared in the bathroom. I was quite upset over it and had to return home without it.

Possibly a year later I returned to my parents' home. While on that visit I noticed my sister Debbie sporting my missing earring. I was so happy she had found it and thanked her as I requested it back. Her response to my request was a flat no. No amount of explanation or pleading would get her to give me back my earring. Her parting words to me were "finders keepers, losers weepers." She was an entitled thief.

My disappointment was huge. I could never steal from anyone let alone openly do it in front of the person I was stealing from. I knew and understood my siblings well growing up. I was beginning to see them as adults and that prospect was frightening. They were drunks, druggies, drug dealers, promiscuous, dishonest and thieves. What else could you expect from the horror show "growing up Zissis,"

My sister Claire had finally let everyone know that she was gay. Her life eerily mirrored my hell. Claire was being "kept" by a local pool parlor owner, enamored with her. She had plenty of money, credit cards, a new stereo and access to the pool parlor owner's car.

At one point I confronted my mother with what was taking place with my underage sister and my mother was uninterested. Claire was about to embark on a journey intended to end with her death.

133

She had been kidnapped by two truckers, while she was in possession of a gun. The kidnappers quickly relieved her of her weapon, and it became their encouragement for my sister to comply with her kidnappers demands. While driving across country, the two-armed men raped my sister for days on end.

I'm not certain how she managed her escape, but she did and hitchhiked all the way back to California from the Midwest. When she arrived home, she told our mother what had happened to her. My mother's response was, "serves you right!"

I honestly can't understand the dismissive attitude of my mother. I would have been worried sick if my child were missing for days on end. Then, if I knew something horrible had happened to them, would try and secure as much help as I could enlist.

I cannot get inside my mother's head, and she is gone now. It just seems odd and incongruent to not want to investigate nor help a child psychologically recover as much as possible. I would as a parent be forever changed by these types of experiences my children were going through. My mother either didn't care or just didn't care to know. Knowing something might require a proper response. A need to step in and help in some way. Any positive response would have been better than the "nothing "response we all received.

We did not share our horror stories with our father at all and neither did our mother. The less he was involved the better. There was no predicting what level of involvement he might have taken. He could have been capable of killing someone. I suspect he would be more apt to lecture us before he turned and walked away though.

These kinds of dysfunctional encounters my siblings and I had are enough to cause a parent a nervous breakdown and/or the desire to play Ostrich. In our circumstances the Ostrich won. It seemed no one cared what happened to any of us. Just as our lives were when we were very young and stayed consistent throughout our lives, we were on our own.

Without God, we were all going to die young. Three of my siblings did die, untimely deaths. My older brother David, my sister Maree and my brother Philip all died in motor vehicle accidents. Maree was pregnant at the time. A tragic loss of life and family.

around the truth and avoiding being real or tolerating and defending abusive behavior. It doesn't mean pretending everything is fine and never questioning secrets and lies. Lastly, it does not mean covering up substance abuse.

In my family everyone of these rules or guidelines were violated. The most egregious violation was me being sworn to secrecy about everything that happened in our home. Boundaries are very difficult to set when you have lived your life in fear. That if you upset anyone, the response would be immediate anger and they would turn on you or completely reject you.

My mother's favorite phrase was "shame on you." She used it to bully everyone into submission. It worked well because most of the time she got her way. I recall a holiday visit to my family's home one Thanksgiving. I was only going to be there for a few short days. It had been a twenty-four-hour drive to get there. We were exhausted from driving straight through and hoped for some much-needed rest and relaxation visiting with my family.

My mother comes up with many ways to use my services and skills while I'm visiting there. Truthfully on this visit I did not care to take on any of my mother's chores, errands or projects. I had not been there long when she handed me a pile of note cards and a box of cut-out recipes. She asked me to type all her recipes onto the individual index cards. This was absolutely nothing I cared to do; however you just don't say no to my mother.

I allowed myself to feel all the feelings attached to my mother's demands. I call them demands because it was expected that you do as you told. For the first time ever, I told her NO. My reason for saying no to her was that I didn't want to do it, plain and simple. Her immediate reaction was to tell me "Shame on me," and next, how "mean and selfish" I was.

She was right about my being selfish. I was determined to do so. I was not going to cave into her shame and criticism. I got my power back. I did not let her verbal assault change my mind. I had won, but the win came at a cost. She gave me the silent treatment for about a year.

James 4:17
For whoever knows the right thing to do and fails to do it, for him it is sin.

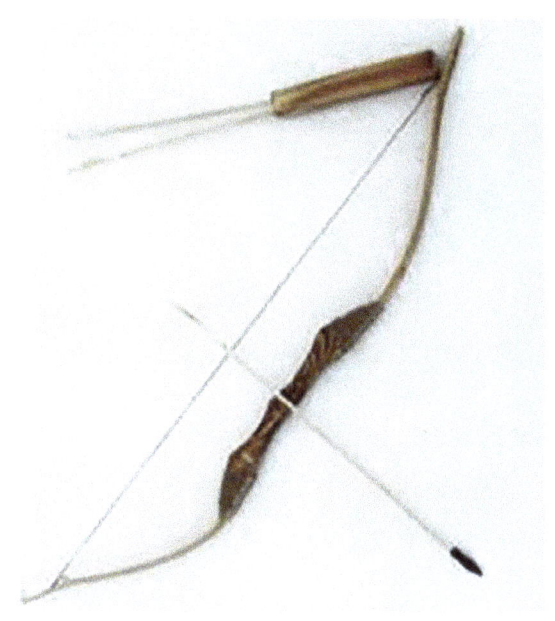

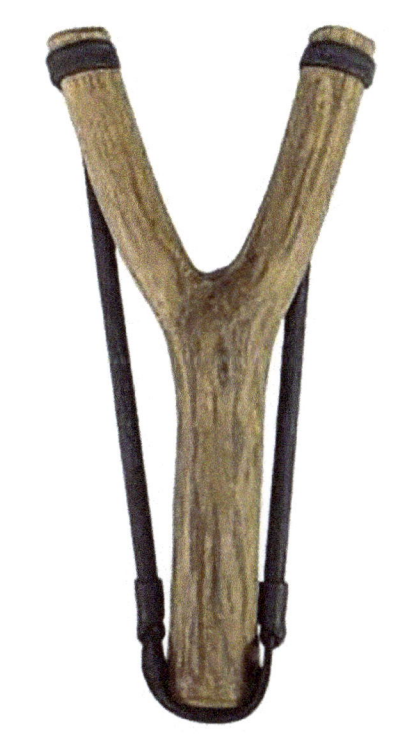

The only picture taken of all eight of us in a room together.
1987.

THE OTHER "F" WORD

"Forgiveness" is God's medicine. It heals our soul and puts us back in the right relationship with our Father. Only God can heal our guilty past. Through forgiveness, God repositions us and points us towards the future and the cross, with God's steady hand.

1 John 3:19-20
This then is how we know we belong to truth, and how we set our hearts to rest in His presence whenever our hearts condemn us. For God is greater than our hearts, and He knows everything.

Forgiveness does not undo the damage or minimize our pain. Nothing is swept under the rug through forgiveness, not our conduct or consequences. Under the rug will cause us to trip up on them at a later date. Forgiveness involves facing feelings and dealing with them honestly. It requires acknowledging the basis for our anger, hurt, guilt and shame. Our feelings which change daily, can lead and teach us to anchor ourselves to God and His Word, because that never changes.

God's mercy allows us to be forgiving. If you don't feel like you deserve forgiveness, that's because you don't deserve it. Forgiveness is a free gift from God, purchased by His blood shed on the cross. We must however make the choice to accept forgiveness. If we refuse that forgiveness, we negate all that He did on the cross on our behalf. It minimizes His suffering, death and ultimate resurrection.

Isaiah 38:7
You have put my sins behind your back.

Knowing and feeling you are forgiven are two very different things. Neither one has anything to do with faith. When we know something, that involves our brain and how we are thinking. Feelings involve our heart and the way we view the world within and around us. Feelings can be faulty.

Satan loves to produce doubt in our hearts and minds, along with God's Word and His intentions for us. If he can convince us that we do not know something, then we begin to doubt everything. Satan's weapon of choice in waging war against us is our emotions.

God's forgiveness is a gift. Just because we don't feel it doesn't mean we didn't get it, that's where confidence and belief in the Word serves us. Feelings are flighty and fickle. God's Word is dependable, sure and never changes.

When we forgive, we are not forgetting. It's impossible to turn off our memory. Excuse is not forgiveness either. Forgiveness is hard, excusing is easy. Accepting is not forgiveness. We accept when things and people are good. We forgive when those same things are bad. We are not simply tolerating behaviors and situations when we choose forgiveness. Tolerating produces conflict and ends with lots of trouble. Forgiveness heals. "Us."

Forgiveness has been the basis and reason behind my "Living Hope" ministry. I've struggled terribly with forgiveness my entire life. After my abortion, I became certifiably unforgivable. I was doomed to hell where I belonged. I committed murder. In my mind there is nothing more egregious I could have done. I did not know that sin is sin. There isn't a sin scale that applies more or less severity to sin depending on what it is.

Going to church was painful with my guilt. I did believe God died on the cross for all sinners, that just didn't happen to include me. I was always emotionally stuck in the same situation. Always a bad person.

Always face the cross when you are "forgiving", and it can't hurt if you're on your knees.

Jeremiah 31:34
For I will forgive their wickedness and will remember no more. When you choose forgiveness always face the cross. This is something I learned many years ago, and it lives in my emotional toolbox.

Forgiveness, summarized:

F-Forgive the hurt done to you.
O-Offer up your confession to Jesus for your sins.
R-Recognize those you have injured.
G-Actively shows love and bless those you are forgiving.
I-Ask God to bless those you are forgiving.
V-Value, in prayer, your enemies believing Christ can change them.
E-Embrace God's forgiveness and rejoice!

FORGIVENESS

AUTHOR UNKNOWN

To forgive is not to forget.
To forgive is really to remember,
That nobody is perfect.

That each of us stumbles,
When we want so much to stay upright.
That each of us says things,
We wish we had never said.
That we can all forget the being right,
That we can all forget that love is more than being right.

To forgive is to remember,
That we are so much more than our mistakes.
That we are often kinder and more caring.
That accepting each other's flaws,
Can help us accept our own.

To forgive is to remember.
That the odds are pretty good,
That soon we may need to be forgiven ourselves.
That life sometimes gives us more,
Than we can handle gracefully.

To forgive is to remember.
That we have room in our hearts to begin again,
And again and again and again.

FORGIVE AGAIN AND AGAIN.

ABIDING IN CHRIST

1 John 2:17

Ａnd the world is passing away along with it's desires, but whoever does the will of God, abides forever.

As our walk matures in Christ, we have choices before us. As we choose now to abide in Christ, it is as living in Him, continuing and/or remaining in Him. When someone comes to the Lord, it is said, they are being "in Christ." The difference between those abiding in Christ and those who are not is the difference between believers and unbelievers. You can only serve one master as they say. You are either serving Christ or you are doing Satan's bidding. I choose Christ continuously and abundantly. This is cleansing and healing to my soul.

Romans 8:1

There is therefore now no condemnation to them which are in Christ Jesus, who walk not after the flesh, but after the Spirit. Abiding in Christ is synonymous with "knowing" Christ. Remaining in the Father is having the promise of eternal life. "Abiding in", "remaining in" and "knowing" Christ are references to the same thing: salvation.

1 John 2:5-6

But if anyone obeys His Word, love for God is truly made complete in them. This is how we know we are in Him: whoever claims to live in Him, must live as Jesus did.

The phrase "abiding in Christ" describes an intimate close relationship and not just a superficial acquaintance. Jesus explained to His disciples, that drawing life from Him is essential, using the picture of branches united to a vine. Believers are the branches of the vine. When we choose Christ, we become the living body and branches of the vine.

John 15:4
Abide in me and I in you. As the branch cannot bear fruit of itself, except it abide in the vine, no more can ye, except ye, abide in me.

When we choose to abide in the Lord and He in me, I bear much fruit. Apart from God, I am nothing. If we choose not to abide in the Lord, we are thrown away as a branch that dries up and then is cast into the fire to burn. Without that vital union with Christ that salvation provides, there can be no life. If we abide in Him and I in you, ask and it will be done.

This being one of the proofs and indicators of salvation, is perseverance or sustained abiding in Christ. Abiding is not what saves us, but it is one of the signs of salvation. The saved will continue their walk in Christ. They will "abide" or remain in Him. God will complete His work in me, and you, and that will bring much fruit to the glory of God.

Revelation 2:26
For the one who is victorious and does My will to the end, I will give authority over the nations.

Philippians 1:6
And I am certain the God who began a great work within you, will continue His work until it is finally finished on the day when Jesus Christ returns.

Proof of abiding in Christ includes obedience to Christ's commands. Living free from habitual sin and an awareness of the divine presence within one's life. Participation as much as possible in corporate worship and fellowship with other like- minded believers.

John 15:10
If you keep my commandments, you will remain in my love, just as I have kept my Father's commands and remain in His love.

1 John 4:13
This is how we know that we live in Him and He in us. He has given us His Spirit.

Abiding in Christ brings my heart peace and security, as well as a way to leave the world behind, giving one's soul over to Christ's capable and willing hands. I choose to rest, abiding in Him. It is my source of renewal. It is where God teaches me.

John 8:31-36
Then Jesus said to those Jews who believed Him, "If you abide in My word, you are My disciples indeed. And you shall know the truth, and the truth shall make you free." They answered Him, "We are Abraham's descendants, and have never been in bondage to anyone. How can You say, 'You will be made free'?" Jesus answered them, "Most assuredly, I say to you, whoever commits sin is a slave of sin. And a slave does not abide in the house forever, buta son abides forever. Therefore, if the Son makes you free, you shall be free indeed.

MOM DIED

I had my mom move to my state, into my complex, right across the hall from me. She did not drive, and I could not care for her three states away. No one else in the family wanted to deal with her. My brother had been trying for years but he was finished. She is emotionally challenging to handle, and my brother and his wife tried for 18 years. The day my mother arrived I picked her up at the airport. She would be staying with me until an apartment became available.

I live in 600 sq. ft. It was going to be challenging. She was not in my home for 10 minutes when she began to cry. I asked her what was wrong, and she said no one wanted her. She was technically correct, no one did. I was included in that except she was now in my home. I pointed out the obvious. "Mom, you're here with me because I wanted you."

I'd decided to look after my mother when no one else would. It wasn't because I loved the idea, it was because God called me to do it. I was trying to do the right thing despite my feelings. I'm a lot of things and wear a lot of hats. Surely, I've not mastered any role yet. I am a Christian. Not a good one, just a forgiven one.

I drove her everywhere and ran her errands for six years. I also worked hard at not being codependent with her. Whenever I was taking care of myself and maintaining boundaries my mother called my sister who threatened to turn me in for elder abuse.

It was emotionally draining to care for her. She made it exceptionally difficult for me. Our church deaconess from time to time would notice me spinning out of control and hand me a book on codependency. I eagerly read them. I needed all the insight and support I could receive.

My mother was a master manipulator and shamed me at every opportunity. I was her least favorite child and her firstborn. She did not care for me because I was too inquisitive and asked too many questions. That was very threatening to a family with lots of secrets. I vowed to never say to my children the words, "shame on you," and never did.

The way I was handled in my family was with put-downs, embarrassment, and made to feel dumb. It made perfect sense that I became an underachiever. I understood my place in the world.

The day my mother died, I woke at 5:30 am and hurried to her apartment. She had been ill and was not expected to live. She had round-the-clock nursing care. I was there whenever my sister Debbie wasn't. I had not put on pajamas in over a week. Earlier she was in the hospital and released from hospice to die at home. I was on a 24-hour call and needed to be in my street clothes at all times.

The nurse on call said my mother had slept all night. I knew that wasn't normal. We checked on her about every fifteen minutes. At about 6:30 the nurse went in and said my mother had passed. I crawled into her bed and laid on top of her crying hysterically. I stayed there for three hours crying.

My daughters called asking me to get off grandma. My ex-husband even called to say I should get off my mother. The nurse was worried I might need an ambulance. I was inconsolable. I tell this story, and everyone assumes I was grieving my mother's death. I was glad my mother had left this world. For my sake and hers. Her life had been cruel for her. My life with my mother had been cruel to me even though I did love her.

What my sorrow was about was quite simply the loss of a dream. The dream and hope that my mother would ever say she loved me. Or was ever going to thank me for all I had done for her and ever hold me with love and appreciation? That ship had sailed.

Logically, it was not likely ever going to happen while she was alive but an unrealistic part of me still hoped for it. I often miss my mother. That is surprising to me. She left her money to my alcoholic sister who lives 2,000 miles away and has never lifted a finger to help my mother. I didn't care about the money. I cared about the intentional statement it made.

My mother wasn't going to give me the satisfaction of knowing I was loved and appreciated even in her death. A truly sentimental gesture.

My niece, who is woefully unaware, actually told me I should get into therapy and try to discover why my mother didn't leave me anything. It was an unfortunate statement made out of ignorance.

Exodus 20:12
Honor your father and mother.

Leviticus 19:3
Every one of you shall revere his mother and father.

My mother as a baby with my grandmother.

My mother a few years before her death.

THE CHOICE FOR JOY

We are always faced with choices to make in life. Sometimes hourly, daily or minute by minute. Many times, the choices we make will set the tone for our future. It is important to weigh choices carefully and soberly.

It doesn't seem possible in the face of tragedy, trauma and abuse to be bold enough to say I'll choose joy. We might not always feel joyous, but we cannot base everything on feelings. Those feelings can often betray us, especially when they are based on faulty thinking.

Feelings are not good or bad, they simply are how we feel. We own them and need to be responsible for how we handle them. Even God's Word cautions us on our feelings. Many religions are founded on feelings. This is a dangerous precedence. It's where one can be easily ensnared by Satan.

1 Peter 1:6-7
In this you rejoice, though now for a little while, if necessary, you have been grieved by various trials, so that the tested genuineness of your faith—more precious than gold that parishes though it is tested by fire—may be found to resuming praise and glory and honor at the revelation of Jesus Christ.

We can spend many days of our lives weighed down with responsibilities and obligations. We move through our day robotically, accomplishing one task after another. We cook, clean, shop, or have a demanding employer to satisfy. We often overextend ourselves with commitments made to others and our day becomes clogged like a log jam. This barely allows an opportunity for us to even lift our heads and take in the day and notice what is taking place in the world around us.

A moment of joy in our day is important to remind us of our circumstances and our hearts. That moment of joy can help us to relax and receive some pleasure from what is good in our daily lives. We must make a conscious decision to look past our minutiae and responsibilities and glimpse God's presence and joy in all things.

Joy and beauty are even in troubling scenarios. God is Omni present, and we can find Him in all situations and things. Satan would have us convinced otherwise, making it difficult to see beauty even in ashes. Everything is created by God, making it beautiful because it was formed by His hand, in His miraculous fashion.

God's Word has many verses of joy and messages of faith along with direction and encouragement for living. Bible verses help us to cultivate a spirit of joy and gratitude. They train us to seek and find joy. Joy should be a regular part of your day.

This does not mean we can't be honest with God in our trials, disappointments, and suffering. God already knows our circumstances and our hearts in all situations.

He expects to hear from you and lament your struggles to Him. This is especially prevalent and taught to us throughout the Psalms. God wants to hear from you regarding your entire journey to be at His side. He created you to love and trust Him.

God is forever our joy, solace, forgiving companion, and confidant. He is our ONLY hope for genuine love and eternal salvation. No one else exists who can make that claim and cause it to happen according to His Word.

Psalm 32:7-11
You are my hiding place; you will protect me from trouble and surround me with songs of deliverance. I will instruct you and will teach you in the way you should go; I will counsel you with my loving eye on you.

John 15:10-12
If you keep my commandments, you will abide in my love, just as I have kept my Father's commandments and abide in His love. These things I have spoken to you, that my joy may be in you, and that your joy may be full. This is my commandment, that you love one another, as I have loved you.

Your life will be richer if you take joy in those you love and the things in life you love doing. Joy is a choice, but the originator of true joy is always the Lord.

Making a decision to respond to life's difficulties and trials with acceptance and contentment is to make a choice for joy. It seems impossible as tribulations hardly seem to be a time of joy. Our gratefulness can be the fact that in our trials we are never left alone. God is with us in every situation, everyday.

James 1:2
My brethren, count it all joy when you fall into various trials.

Is it really possible to have joy during trials? It is a process of learning to respond with joy during times of trials and it must begin with a conscious awareness that God is at work and in charge in your life. God has a tangible reason and purpose why we are experiencing difficulties that He is working out. During difficult times in our lives, God has a specific purpose or lesson in mind. He is growing us as children of God. We are being educated by the best parent, dedicated to seeing we receive our inheritance of eternal life with Him.

Romans 10:9
If you declare with your mouth, "Jesus is Lord," and believe in your heart that God raised Him from the dead, you will be saved.

Philippians 2:13
For it is God who works in you to will and to act in order to fulfill His good purpose.

We can respond to life's trials by hearing God's Word and promises and understand that trials produce patience and endurance, along with the ability to weather storms. We will be held up under the weight of trials in our lives, as we cling to God and His Word. In our trials and times of feeling alone, we can cling to the promise that we are actually never alone. God is always in charge of everything. That is a reason to celebrate and experience joy in all circumstances.

God made us with the ability to choose. We can choose joy in our lives also. Make it a daily habit. Allow God to place joy in your life and give you the eyes to see and appreciate it.

Embrace joy, joyously. Seek it in all things. It doesn't matter if you're sad and/or alone. Joy is there if you allow it to be. It's one of God's blessed provisions for us. Seek and God will bless you with joy.

If you try and cannot find any joy, simply remember who is with you at all times, never leaving your side. To have that kind of friend who is also your Father, teacher, the one who consoles you, defends you, weeps for you and celebrates you in infinite ways is gloriously comforting. How can a special love so true and pure not bring you some measure of joy?

GOD IN CHARGE

We are completely dependent on God every moment in order to stay alive. The Bible tells us we are only alive because He keeps us breathing. God is in charge of preserving everyone's life. He is the author and creator of the universe. He is always looking out for our best interests.

Psalm 42:8
The Lord will command His loving kindness in the daytime: and His song will be with me in the night, a prayer to God for my life.

Job 12:10
In whose hand is the life of everything, and the breath of all mankind?

Psalm 66:9
You have kept us alive and not allowed us to fall.

God sees all and understands everything from His perspective and ours. However, we do not have all the answers and need God for strength and ultimately our salvation. Without God, salvation does not belong to us. No matter how great one's power, wealth, or dignity, one can be by God's power, reduced to nothing before Him. We need the Lord in all situations and areas of our life.

Trying to go it alone is daunting. We will stumble and fall and not always know how to get back up. God is in our corner. He sees and knows what we struggle with. He is there to guide us back on our feet so that we can continue the journey with Him. He never leaves our side.

Isaiah 40:23
He brings princes to naught and rulers of this world to nothing.

So God warns us and kings and rulers to be careful as He judges the earth. He is in control. God's sovereignty is an essential part of who He is. God has supreme authority and absolute power over all things. And He is very much active despite the fact that we can always rely on God to answer our prayer requests. We just have to be willing to accept His Godly answer.

Ephesians 1:11
In Him, we are also chosen having been predestined according to the plan of Him who works out everything in conformity to His plan.

Psalm 115:3
Our God is in the heavens, He does all things He pleases.

God is in control of all things in Heaven and Earth and makes sure to do what is best for us at all times.

He intimately knows our needs, desires, and our hearts. That does not mean that God does not want us to choose according to His will out of obedience. He wants us to make our decisions out of His blueprint. It is the Holy Spirit who guides our choices as we have the freedom to make them. God's sovereignty is His right to do all things according to His good pleasure.

Colossians 1:16-17
For by Him all things were created in Heaven and on earth, visible and invisible, whether thrones or dominions or rulers or authorities,

all things were created through Him and for Him. And He is before all things and in Him all things hold together. We should take heart in the knowledge that God is miraculously in charge and worry not, nor fear for anything.

I was asked to tell my suicide story to thousands of people. It is the most amazing story. There is no logical explanation for why I am alive except that God had other plans. I wrote and delivered the speech two years after the event. The story lives on, filmed in a full auditorium on Facebook and YouTube.

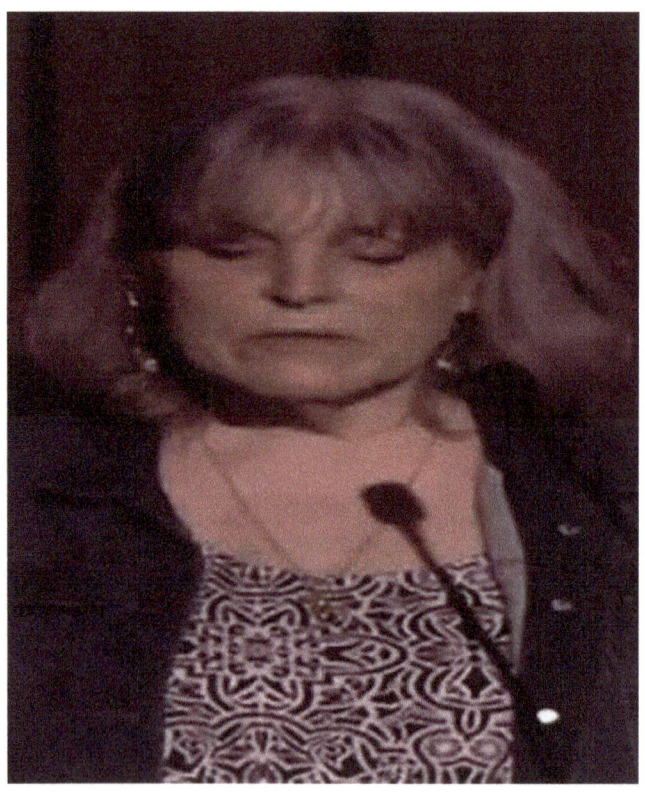

Speech day. November 5, 2020
I now permanently reside on U-tube.

A LETTER TO MY YOUNGER SELF

I'm so glad to know you and have deep admiration for you. I particularly admire how you changed your story along with your journey from that of victim to being your own co-hero. I'm so sorry your childhood required you to grow up faster and become a more serious child. You should have been able to play the days away as a little girl. Your childhood should not have been a burden placed on your tiny shoulders that was too great for you. The weight of that burden kept you down in ways you're just now learning about. You deserved to be loved, protected and free from the abuses you endured.

You have admirably turned devastating losses into gains that have transformed your heart. You possess an undeniable resilience, even on the darkest days. You've adapted well in the face of adversity, trauma, tragedy, threats and significant stress. I'm glad you have the inner fortitude to keep going. It's not always easy but you're here.

You have the ability to always hold onto hope that something better is just around the corner and the worst does not ever stop you. I admire your strength; you're caring for others and generosity towards people. You possess courage and wisdom that can only come from a life begun in sorrow and pain. You made a brave choice to seek God and ask Him to heal and save your soul. God is our Healer and Savior.

Your sadness is also where your strengths and understanding of others' pain comes from. You have walked in other people's shoes, just as Christ has experienced everyone's pain. It is often difficult for people to relate to ongoing long-term pain, suffering and repeated crisis to someone who has never come close to receiving trauma and abuse.

You have chosen peace and growth over the inner drama you faced in your daily life. That helps to stop the regression back to your previous unsteady and unpredictable self. You have always sought growth over stagnation. God has blessed you in so many ways and you see His work over and over in your life.

I've come to respect and love you. You are forever a poor miserable beggar and sinner before Christ. I really do like you now. More often than not, the clouds are lifted, and you consciously feel yourself reconnecting again. It's the feeling that stops the negative talk in your head and drowns out all the negative voices there too.

You are fully able to believe in God as your Father and do not distrust or second guess Him as you did yourself along with your earthly father and stepfather. It is only by God's grace that these positive transformations have taken place and continue to do so. God is the ultimate healer and teacher. All glory and honor belong to Him.

A single individual can't change their life so drastically on their own without God's intervention. He is all-powerful in that regard and rightfully deserves all the glory and honor. You have been blessed so mercifully that it continues to humble your heart. You have been granted a gift more precious than gold. You've been granted a life with Jesus. A love that is strong, genuine, honest, and very real. It is a love that is salvation, wonderful and free.

*If you do not know this kind of love, simply ask Him for it. He longs to lavish you in it. He hears your every cry and wants to begin the process of healing your life and your soul. Seek Him genuinely.

1 John 3:1
See what great love the Father has lavished on us, that we should be called children of God. And that is what we are.

A love for us so great, He died.

Kindergarten

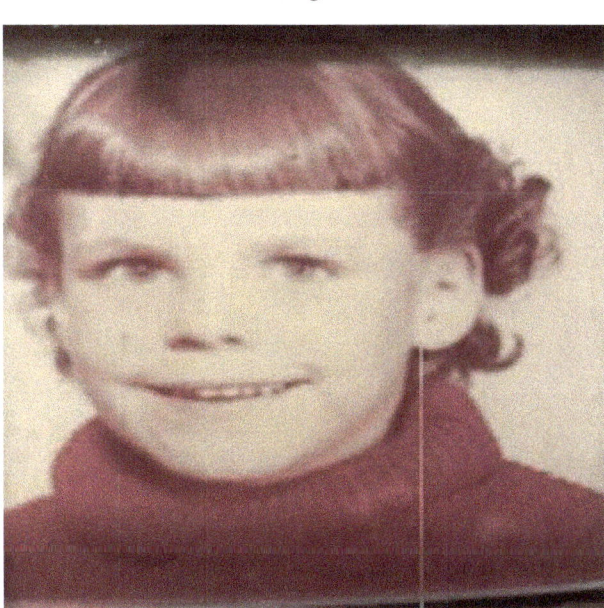

THEY'RE DEAD

Most of the abusers are dead now. That brings me a certain peace. Two are still living and are currently residing in my state. One I occasionally have run into. Doing so is more painful and humiliating than the actual sex abuse was.

I attempted to kill this offender once. I was eleven years old. I planned my attack and followed through only to be stopped by my grandmother, who was aghast at my attempt. She had no idea what or why I was trying to injure my cousin. He wasn't dead but I hoped I'd hurt him just the same. I still wish him dead and in Satan's capable hands.

The state I live in recently lifted its statute of limitations on sex abuse crimes. That leaves me free to pursue these offenders legally. I have prayerfully considered this option as I would love nothing more than to see the judicial consequences befall them. In order to pursue this course of action I have to be willing to become an emotional victim again.

As much as I would love to have retribution for the crimes committed against me, it is a toll on my brain that I'm not willing to undertake. God has the power to deal with justice also. Even though He has provided us courts to do so, it is not the only way justice is served.

So much has been left out of this story. I could spend a lifetime writing the endless escapades of growing up in Zissis. There are 12 siblings in all. I have only one whole sibling. That speaks to the issues at hand. Too many cooks in the kitchen, so they say.

I have one other sibling I'm aware of who is a Christian. She is the only sibling I have any contact with. I've had to take myself out of the blood-related family game. It comes at too high of an emotional price. I love my family and pray for them fervently each day, but I can no longer interact with them. There simply is too much dysfunction for me to cope with.

I'm essentially saving myself. It is how I care for my emotional well-being. I stay out of the fray and fire. It works too. I've enjoyed more substantial well-being by releasing myself from toxic relatives and toxic friends, including one-sided relationships in the past few years than twenty years of therapy accomplished. I certainly gained considerable knowledge and support from therapy but leaving the unhealthy relationships behind accomplished more than I anticipated. I now can fully breathe.

God has blessed my soul in so many ways. He has led me to an important ministry "Living Hope" which ministers to the broken hearts of post-abortive women. Through that ministry, a participant was led by God to open a brick-and-mortar business doing just that, including women and families with all-encompassing reproductive issues and concerns.

God took a seed planted by me (with God's help and encouragement) and grew a mighty forest from it. It now reaches out to many more broken hearts. It is truly a blessing to be able to witness God's handiwork.

The Moline family has watched the seeds that were planted in my heart by their love and support for me over the last 58 years. God understood my need at age twelve and took care of me. He used a blessed, loving, and faithful family to accomplish it.

They never once preached to me. They quite simply lived their faith as servants of Christ.

My life has been a combination of hardships, abuse, terror, redemption, and blessings. I expect more of the same. We are not promised a bed of roses to lie in. We are promised trials and tribulations. Prepare yourself with God's Word. Fortify your heart with Him. Gain strength and wisdom in your relationship with the Father. God has loved me and rescued me from the damage done while a child and the consequences of that damage. He is forever faithful and determined to win your heart through His abundant love.

No matter how committed, sin will always be exposed. God's Word guarantees it.

Luke 12:2
"There is nothing concealed that will not be disclosed or hidden, that will not be known."

PSALM 32
(MY PSALM)

Blessed is the one whose transgressions are forgiven, whose sins are covered.

Blessed is the one whose sin the Lord does not count against them and in whose spirit is no deceit.

When I kept silent, my bones wasted away through my groaning, all day long.

For a day and night, your hand was heavy on me; my strength was sapped as in the heat of summer.

Then I acknowledged my sin to you and did not cover my iniquity. I said, "I will confess my transgressions to the Lord. And you forgave the guilt of my sin.

Therefore, let all the faithful pray to you while you may be found, surely the rising of the mighty waters.

Will not reach them. You are my hiding place; you will protect me from trouble and surround me with songs of deliverance.

I will instruct you and teach you the way you should go; I will counsel you with my loving eye on you.

Do not be like the horse or the mule, which have no understanding but must be controlled by bit and bridle, or they will not come to you.

Many are the woes of the wicked, but the Lord's unfailing love surrounds the one who trusts in him.

Rejoice in the Lord and be glad, you are righteous; sing, all you who are upright in heart!

HOPE

It is a distinct time of hope we are living in. I survive off this gem. It is my mantra. I can believe in hope because the Father promises it to me. I no longer need to exist in perpetual despair. God will always be with me in the darkness, I just don't need the darkness any longer and have a contingency plan to avoid it. This does not mean I don't struggle. It means I get up each time I fall. With courage, I continue on my way once more with humility and hope. Gifts granted from a loving Father.

Our "hope" is in Christ. Because I rely on this, I can proceed calmly knowing God is in control. You see, God does not lose battles. Hope is the upside of sorrow. Without sorrow, we could not appreciate Hope.

Sorrow causes us to evaluate ourselves honestly. We search for our motives and intentions. It offers us an opportunity to know ourselves better. Sorrow draws us closer to God and helps us to see Him as we never have before either. Job spoke out of his horrible grief and sorrow:

Job 42:5
"I have heard of You by hearing of the ear, but now my eye sees You,"

Jesus, perfect in every way was described as a "man of sorrows." He was intimately acquainted with grief.

In Ecclesiastes, it is written, verse 7:3 "Sorrow is better than laughter, for by a sad countenance the heart is made better,"

As we study Christ's sorrow, we can gain a better understanding and appreciation for what God is working to accomplish in us through our trials and grief. It's important to let sorrow do its work. Do not deny it, trivialize it, or try to justify or explain it away.   It's easy to remain shallow and/or simply indifferent about it. GOD always has a plan. Make a way for it.

Without Hope, our confidence diminishes because of self- doubt. That leads us to utter despair and the ultimate darkness. When we embrace self-doubt and judgment with love, we are then drawn like moths to God's sacred light of the soul.

If you need a place to put your Hope, place it in God's Divine Powerful Hands. They will not fail you. Ever! No one is ever hopeless who knows the God and author of hope.

"Jesus did not come to explain away suffering or remove it. He came to fill it with His presence."
Author, Paul Claudel

THANK YOU LORD

Thank you, Lord, for all that goes wrong in our day.
It provides a way and opportunity to sit back and watch You at work.
In Your awesome wonder.

Thank you, Lord, for our illnesses,
it leads us to Your living water and Your healing touch.
And blessings by Your hand.

Thank you, Lord, for the times of unemployment and loss.
It lets us become wholly dependent.
On Your faithfully sustaining ways.

Thank you, Lord, for those who are single or alone.
It allows an opportunity to know a greater love in You.
One with Your intimacy, grace and mercy.

Thank you Lord for every affliction whatever they may be.
We learn from them to depend on Your guidance and Word.
Leaving us needing and wanting You more.

Thank you, Lord, for those who are in need and want.
It allows us the privilege of praying for them,
So that Your will can be done and draws us more closely to You.

Cross in Groom, Texas. Second tallest cross in the USA,
at 190 feet tall.

A self-portrait done at age nineteen.